P9-DXE-894

OPPORTUNITIES

in

Health and Medical Careers

OPPORTUNITIES

in

Health and Medical Careers

REVISED EDITION

LEO PAUL D'ORAZIO AND I. DONALD SNOOK JR.

VGM Career Books

New York   Chicago   San Francisco   Lisbon   London   Madrid   Mexico City
Milan   New Delhi   San Juan   Seoul   Singapore   Sydney   Toronto

The *McGraw·Hill* Companies

Library of Congress Cataloging-in-Publication Data

D'Orazio, Leo.
    Opportunities in health and medical careers / by Leo Paul D'Orazio and I. Donald
Snook, Jr.— Rev. ed.
        p.   cm. — (VGM opportunities series)
    Snook's name appears first on earlier ed.
    ISBN 0-07-143727-4
    1. Medicine—Vocational guidance.   2. Allied health personnel—Vocational
guidance.   I. Snook, I. Donald.   II. Title.   III. Series.

    R690.D67   2004
    610.69—dc22   2004006718

1 2 3 4 5 6 7 8 9 0   DOC/DOC   3 2 1 0 9 8 7 6 5 4

ISBN 0-07-143727-4

Interior design by Rattray Design

McGraw-Hill books are available at special quantity discounts to use as premiums and
sales promotions, or for use in corporate training programs. For more information, please
write to the Director of Special Sales, Professional Publishing, McGraw-Hill, Two Penn
Plaza, New York, NY 10121-2298. Or contact your local bookstore.

This book is printed on acid-free paper.

This revised edition is dedicated to the memory of the book's primary coauthor, I. Donald Snook, who passed away in November 2002. Don was a great health care professional, author, educator, mentor, and friend. Those who were touched by his life will never forget him. I am honored and blessed to be one of those fortunate people.

CONTENTS

technologist/technician. Emergency medical
technician (E.M.T.)/paramedic. Medical laboratory
technologist/technician. Medical physicist.
Microbiologist. Nuclear medicine technologist/
technician. Optician. Optometric technician.
Pharmacist. Pharmacologist. Radiologic (x-ray)
technician.

Administrative roles. Health administration as a
profession. Management and administration in
hospitals. Chief executive officer (CEO)/
administrator. Chief operations officer (COO)/
administrative officer. Chief financial officer (CFO).
Chief nursing officer (CNO). Chief medical officer
(CMO)/medical director. Long-term care/nursing
home administrator. Hospital controller. Director,
patient accounts. Director of admissions. Director of
managed care. Director of human resources.
Purchasing director/materials manager. Food service
administrator. Executive housekeeper. Director of
volunteer services. Care/case manager. Risk manager.
Quality assurance director. Director of planning.
Director of public relations. Director of marketing.
Director of development.

Central service technician. Dietary manager. Dietetic
technician. Hospital engineer. Hospital food service

worker (dietary aide). Hospital housekeeping worker. Hospital laundry worker. Hospital maintenance worker. Medical illustrator. Medical records technician. Registered record administrator.

contents

9. Getting Started in the Health and Medical Professions — 129

Preparing your résumé. The cover letter. Successful interviewing. Follow-up and accepting the job.

contents

Appendix A: Common Medical Abbreviations and Acronyms — 137
Appendix B: Facilities, Services, and Programs Where Health Care Workers Are Employed — 141
Glossary of Selected Health and Medical Terms — 145

FOREWORD

HUMAN BEINGS HAVE always required the services offered by the medical profession, and they always will. The ability of medical practitioners to save lives and relieve suffering places them in the most respected of professions. Further, the steady and tremendous scientific advances made in the field of medicine over the past several hundred years have led us to expect and rely on a quality of care that is unsurpassed.

These advances have expanded the depth and breadth of the medical field. Yet medicine is just a part of the much larger field of health care. The health care field is a complex system that utilizes not only the services of doctors, dentists, ophthalmologists, and the like, but also those of specialists in numerous medical and support areas and countless technicians who operate and service specialized equipment and analyze the results of various tests. Clearly, the opportunities in such an enormous undertaking are many.

But the opportunities do not stop there. Many essential and related nonmedical careers are available to those who are interested in them. Such jobs run the gamut from housekeeping to medical records to public relations.

If you have an interest in medicine and health care, *Opportunities in Health and Medical Careers* will help you explore the many options this exciting field has to offer.

The Editors
VGM Career Books

ACKNOWLEDGMENTS

Special thanks to Raymond J. Thacker, director of marketing and consultant at the McFaul & Lyons Group, for his untiring research abilities.

1

A DIVERSE
AND GROWING FIELD

WHAT WILL HEALTH care and health care employment look like in the twenty-first century? Where there is change there is opportunity, including opportunity for jobs. Thousands of health care jobs are created each month. The U.S. Bureau of Labor Statistics predicts that jobs in health care should grow 47 percent overall by the year 2005. Health care jobs will grow twice as fast as the average for all industries.

Change Abounds in Health Care

One of the most profound changes in the field of health care is the shift away from individual hospitals in favor of multihospital and integrated delivery systems (IDS). This has created new jobs at a corporate level. It is also believed that the development of these multihospital systems will increase the need for specialty managers.

In addition, there has been a dramatic shift in the delivery of health care from hospitals to alternative delivery settings such as outpatient centers and home health and assisted living services.

Inpatient hospital days have decreased by 15 percent to 25 percent, while outpatient procedures have increased by 20 percent to 30 percent. Total hospital revenue will be almost equally divided between in- and outpatient services. However, outpatient revenues are likely to eclipse inpatient revenues. In 2000 some eight hundred regional integrated health care delivery networks accounted for 80 percent of all health care delivered, and this percentage is growing.

A look at the demographics of our country shows that the 65 and older group is the fastest growing population cohort in the U.S. Census. Herein lies a significant demand for long-term care managers in nursing home facilities, continuing care retirement communities, assisted living facilities, and senior housing campuses. The number of managed care organizations will continue to increase, especially in the Medicare managed care business. As in many growth industries, there will be a demand for qualified employees. (See Table 1.1.)

Other fast-growing alternative delivery systems include freestanding surgi-centers, cancer centers, and imaging centers. Where there is such rapid change, there is opportunity for health care employment.

America's health care labor force in the twenty-first century will be more culturally diverse. Many publications and experts have discussed the future trends for the changing workplace. For example, nearly two-thirds of the new entrants in the year 2000 were women, and in that same year 61 percent of all women of working age had jobs.

Table 1.1 Fields with the Greatest Projected Needs, 2004–2005

Occupation	Average Yearly Income	Approximate Number of Jobs by 2005
Dental Assistant	$19,000	264,000
Dental Hygienist	30,000	141,000
Emergency Medical Technician	25,000	50,000
Home Health Aide	11,000	827,000
Licensed Practical Nurse	23,500	1,100,000
Medical Assistant	22,000	310,000
Medical Records Technician	24,000	123,000
Nurse's Aide, Orderly	16,500	1,700,000
Registered Nurse	30,000	2,400,000
Occupational Therapist	35,000	64,000
Occupational Therapy Assistant	20,000	15,000
Optician	24,000	20,000
Personal and Home Care Aide	16,500	290,000
Pharmacist	45,000	200,000
Physical Therapist	30,000	170,000
Physician's Assistant	54,000	42,000
Podiatrist	80,000	15,000
Psychologist	60,000	150,000
Radiological Technician	29,000	220,000
Respiratory Therapist	30,000	180,000
Speech-Communication Pathologist	39,000	12,000

The Needs Continue

The demand for health care service workers continues. The reasons are rooted in the American system of delivering health care:

1. Our citizens have become accustomed to and have learned to expect the very best in health care in the world, but there tends to be an uneven distribution of the health care delivered. As an illustration, note that infant mortality continues to be too high among many minority populations. Within our affluent cities there are

"megacenters of medicine," but a few short blocks away in the same cities one can also find blight and decay, where large numbers of inner-city dwellers—the poor and near-poor—are without proper health services. Add to this the numerous rural areas of the country that lack many rudimentary health services.

2. Our population continues to expand and shift, putting a heavy load on certain health services. With those shifts sometimes comes a decline in the quantity and quality of services. Add to this equation the fact that Americans are living longer, and, therefore, an increased demand for the medical care of the elderly is created. In fact, 80 percent of our health care resources are utilized by 20 percent of our population, mostly the elderly.

3. Medical research continues to relentlessly race on. Medical science has been successful in setting high standards for all in the professions.

4. With the staggering costs of medical care continuing and taking a larger bite out of our country's budget, the nation's health care bill is approximately $1.5 trillion dollars annually. This is approximately 15 percent of the country's gross national product. With these incredible costs, it becomes necessary to target the use of resources more effectively. These resources must become more efficient in rendering health care. This may translate into allowing the higher priced professional personnel, i.e., physicians and registered nurses, to do one set of tasks while less trained people, auxiliary personnel, and paraprofessionals do other tasks. Efficiency is being mandated.

Health Manpower

The single most pressing issue facing health manpower today is whether there is an appropriate supply of the right kind of health professionals and paraprofessionals to meet our needs. Answering this question is not a simple matter. It involves many complex decisions. One thing is clear; change is constantly confronting the medical care system and new health care professionals.

Change is affecting not only the new technology and equipment that are so vital for our health care delivery system, but also the financial and reimbursement systems and new treatment modalities that are being introduced literally every week. These changes are interactive and not only affect health manpower but other resources throughout the health care system as well. Change causes its own problems. Take as an example just how difficult it is to predict with any reliability the exact number of given health professionals needed in the next five or ten years. Let's illustrate by speculating on the number of nurse practitioners needed in the next five years. To estimate, we would have to take into account how many primary care physicians there will be and what their relationship to each other will be, and whether inner cities will continue to deteriorate and whether primary care physicians will move er cities and rural areas. If they do not, then there will for nurse practitioners. If physicians do relocate, ind new markets for their , occupational therapists s in hospitals and nursing s and technicians working aditional settings. Change and it is influencing health

Total items:
You just saved $62.89 by usi
have saved $106.88 this past year and $
ince you began using the library!
Thank You!

ng

The health field offers a vast array of opportunities. If you like working with your hands, there are opportunities as a health management information technician, registered nurse, biomedical equipment technician, or a prosthetics technician, just to name a few. If understanding and working with machines is to your liking, then there are opportunities to work as a radiographer (x-ray technician), respiratory therapist, or as an EKG (electrocardiograph) or EEG (electroencephalograph) technician.

Are you more inclined toward the arts or photography? If so, then the specialties of dance, art, or music therapy are available. If you want to work directly with people every day, then perhaps nursing, social work, or medicine would be in your future.

It is important to note the difference between education in a university or a college and training that is often done in a nonuniversity setting. There are the two avenues open to health professionals and workers. Training in our system usually involves an effort to prepare a person for a given specific occupation or position. There is a great deal of emphasis on pragmatic learning skills with an orientation to tasks rather than to theory. Training is founded on a narrower framework than education. Training offers fewer opportunities to explore related information and material. Education, on the other hand, stresses an understanding beyond just performing a task. Education is interested in linkages between disciplines. Education seeks out a greater breadth of knowledge. Education for the health professional frequently includes a study of economic conditions and psychological, social, cultural, and historical perspectives.

The Government's Role

Education and training are intricately involved with the federal government's allocation of money to manpower development. It appears that the federal government believes that more money is not necessary to prime the health professional's education and training pump. There are fewer financial incentives available now than in the past. Recent reductions in funding for nursing schools have met with a large outcry from nursing faculty members and organized nursing in general. This is predictable when a professional educational program relies too heavily on federal and governmental dollars. It is fair to say that if the government continues to cut back on its incentives for health education and training, then the cutback will not be evenly distributed and certain occupations will feel the sting of the cutback more than others will.

Continuing Education

As medical research continues to expand its horizon and new technological gadgets are found to aid in diagnosis and treatment, old and once-reliable medical procedures become obsolete. With these new procedures, there is a need for more highly specialized training. For example, new advances in heart surgery demand that operating room personnel be up to date in the latest techniques. Also, for men and women who have been out of the health care occupation or professional activity for years, it may be necessary to take refresher courses—programs that are formal and frequently short-term—to recapture lost skills and become informed on today's advanced knowledge. Continuing education offers society proof that the professional is competent to meet the health care standards in the profession. In short, the concept of continuing education in the health care field is a common and critical component in the work life of health care providers.

2

The Medical Care System

HEALTH CARE WORKERS are employed or independently in practice within health service and medical care systems in this country. *Webster's* defines a system as a set or arrangement of things so related or connected as to form a unity or organic whole. More specifically, the health system or medical care system is a set of mechanisms through which human resources, health care facilities, and medical technology are organized by means of administrative structures. The medical care system offers integrated services in sufficient quantity and quality to meet the community's demands at a cost compatible with the community's financial resources. The American medical care system has five distinct elements. Four of these elements or components are related to specific institutions; the fifth element, i.e., the community at large, encompasses or surrounds these institutions. Let us examine each of the components and institutions with which the medical care system is associated.

Outreach Component

Perhaps the best place to start our review of the medical care system is with the outreach component. It is a general rule of thumb in this country that the traditional medical care system attempts to meet the primary medical care needs of its patients through outreach programs. These programs are generally decentralized and widely scattered. One of the earliest and most common types of outreach services is the solo medical practitioner, with offices located in neighborhoods. Physicians with private practices provide the bulk of care to the middle class in this country, but the urban poor continue to use city health clinics and similar institutions as a substitute for family physicians. Other forms of the outreach component include neighborhood community health centers, community mental health agencies, physician group practices, and a variety of other ambulatory care arrangements, including the outreach activities of health maintenance organizations (HMOs).

Hospitals also have reached out into their communities and demonstrated a new emphasis on preventive care by adding or expanding health promotion services. These educational and support services are intended to help individuals learn how to reduce health risks, manage health, and use health services effectively. They may be targeted at patients through patient education services, or at residents of the community who are not currently patients.

Outpatient Component

Another area of our medical care system is outpatient care. One of the major institutions providing this component is the traditional hospital clinic. The growing outpatient services also include emergency facilities. Large numbers of patients continue to steadily use emergency rooms across this country. Included in the outpatient component are ambulance squads, whether they are community, municipal, or police or firefighter rescue squads. Ambulance assistance is an outpatient service that has taken on increased status with the advent of paramedics, emergency medical technicians (EMTs), and emergency medical systems, such as the cardiopulmonary resuscitation teams that have saved so many lives. Physician group practices are common in larger medical centers and are also included in this outpatient category.

Even more dramatic than the decline in inpatient hospital use has been the increase in community hospital outpatient visits. The increased volume of surgical procedures being done on an outpatient basis accounts for much of the growth in outpatient visits. The shift toward ambulatory surgery is not the only factor behind growth in hospital outpatient visits. Community hospitals have expanded the number and variety of outpatient services they provide.

Inpatient Component

The third institutional component and the largest in terms of cost and personnel is the inpatient component. The inpatient element is measured by the number of hospital beds. Americans have asked the country's hospitals to provide a spectrum of inpatient care ranging from very sophisticated intensive care to minimal care, all of these types of care taking place within the hospital walls using hospital beds. The inpatient component is the most costly in the system. Over the past decade, inpatient activity at community hospitals has fallen while the use of hospital outpatient services has increased dramatically. Many treatments and procedures that would have required an inpatient stay ten years ago are now routinely delivered in outpatient settings. As a result, fewer patients are being admitted to hospitals.

Hospitals vary by ownership, purpose, and specialty. The most common hospital is the short-term community hospital. There are more than 4,900 community hospitals. Hospitals operated by governments, whether state, federal, city, county, or district, are called governmental or municipal hospitals. There is a third category, referred to as specialty hospitals, which includes long-term care hospitals.

Extended Component

This is the fourth element in the medical care system. Included in the extended component, but not limited to it, are such services and institutions as home health care and hospice programs, end-stage renal disease programs, skilled nursing facilities (SNFs), and intermediate care facilities (ICFs). Together the SNFs and the ICFs are referred to as nursing homes. There are also assisted living facilities, personal care residences, rehabilitation hospitals, visiting nurses associations, and a more recent phenomenon called hospice care.

This extended component is expanding in breadth of services due mainly to the growth in the elderly and poor populations, both of which tend to suffer frequently from chronic conditions. This has resulted in a shift in focus from episodes of illness (such as admissions, visits, or length of stays) to continuous, comprehensive care management.

Community-at-Large Component

The fifth and final element in the medical care system is the non-institutional component referred to as the community at large. The community is divided into three major groups. The first is composed of the consumers—the patients who use the health care facilities. The second group is composed of the health personnel needed to staff the system. This includes a variety of training programs and medical and nursing schools, as well as medicine's residency programs. Also included in this element are labor unions. Third, and perhaps the most powerful part of the community component, is the federal government, which pays for so much of the hospital care through the Medicare and Medicaid programs. The private insurance company or industry provides coverage for the majority of employed Americans. Key elements under the community at large are the federal, state, local, and voluntary regulatory agencies. Much of the regulatory controls are focused on quality care and cost issues. Finally, the political system, the politics of health care, drives much of the legislation that governs the funding and direction of the health care system in this country.

In this outline of the five distinct components that make up our nation's medical care system one thing is very clear. The system tends to be a sickness-care system more than a health care system. With the growth in managed care organizations, this is starting to change. Each of the medical care components is part of a complex array of institutions and programs that involve people and countless other resources.

3

PHYSICIANS/DOCTORS
AND ASSISTANTS

THE PRACTICE OF healing is one of the oldest professions, yet today's medicine has changed a great deal from even a decade ago. Many of the aspects of traditional medical practice have changed. Physicians are responding to new demands on time, advances in drugs, and increased technology and equipment, as well as therapeutic techniques. These changes have contributed to the creation of a variety of additional jobs that directly support the physician.

In this country there are close to 836,156 physicians who are divided into a variety of specialties. There is the general practice of family physicians, pediatrics, obstetrics, and gynecology. Included in this physician group are doctors of osteopathy. A physician also could practice one of more than 22 medical specialties or subspecialties. For example, radiologists are involved in taking patient x-rays and reading them. General surgeons diagnose and perform surgery on patients with surgical problems. Cardiologists work with patients who have heart problems.

Another old and respected profession is dentistry. The more than 150,000 dentists and their dental staffs are committed to treating and diagnosing problems of the mouth, gums, and teeth. Prevention has been one of the key objectives in the dental profession.

Yet another area is that of podiatry, which involves the care of the foot. The more than six thousand podiatrists are doctors professionally trained in foot care. They are involved in all aspects of treating the foot, including the diagnosis, prevention, and treatment of medical and surgical foot problems.

Assistants, too, play a major role in supporting physicians in providing medical care. The following list of professions and occupations provides an overview of the jobs that bear directly on a physician's practice.

Chiropractor

Chiropractors practice a unique area of health care known as *chiropractic*. Chiropractic is believed to be based on the nervous system, which in turn oversees physical health. Therefore, chiropractors rely on the belief that the nervous system controls disorders of the body. Chiropractors manipulate body parts, especially the spinal column, which in turn is the major source for the nervous system. Chiropractors do not use drugs or surgery to treat their patients.

• **Educational Requirements.** A four-year training program in a chiropractic school is required. Students receive a degree of Doctor of Chiropractic (D.C.). All states require practitioners to be licensed. Students generally need at least two years of college before they can enroll.

• **The Need.** Job prospects are expected to be good. Employment is expected to grow faster than the average for all occupations through the year 2012. Chiropractors usually remain in the occupation until they retire; few transfer to other occupations.

- **Number in the Field.** 65,000
- **Salaries.** Starting salaries are approximately $55,000 per year. The average is between $80,000 and $90,000 per year. Some can earn more than $220,000 per year.

For further information write:

American Chiropractic Association
1701 Clarendon Boulevard
Arlington, VA 22209
amerchiro.org

Dental Assistant

A dental assistant works as a receptionist and secretary in a dentist's office. He or she may also serve as a chair-side assistant, perform laboratory work, take dental x-rays, provide instruction in oral hygiene, and prepare and sterilize instruments. A dental assistant must have knowledge of basic business procedures, the ability to follow instructions, and a friendly, tolerant personality.

Dental assistants work in dentists' offices, clinics, dental schools, and local health agencies. Also, they may work in insurance companies, processing claims.

- **Educational Requirements.** One year of training in theory and clinical application with work experience in dental offices is required. Most states require that you pass the examination given by the Certifying Board of the American Dental Assistant's Association. Associate's degree programs for dental assistants are also available.

• **The Need.** Job prospects for dental assistants are excellent. Dental assistant is expected to be one of the fastest-growing occupations through the year 2012. Many opportunities are for entry-level positions, which offer on-the-job training.
  • **Number in the Field.** 225,000
  • **Salaries.** The average salary for a dental assistant is $26,000.

For further information write:

American Dental Assistant's Association
35 East Wacker Drive, Suite 1730
Chicago, IL 60601
dentalassistant.org

Dental Hygienist

A dental hygienist cleans and polishes teeth and charts the condition of an individual's teeth and gums for treatment by a dentist. The hygienist also teaches groups and individuals the proper care of teeth and the mouth. Dental hygienists should have excellent vision and good manual dexterity, as they work in small areas with delicate tools. A sincere interest in people and a warm personality will help in dealing with patients.

Dental hygienists work in dentists' offices, clinics, public schools, and local health agencies. They also can pursue careers in office management, business administration, dental hygiene education, and research and marketing of dental-related materials and equipment.

• **Educational Requirements.** Graduation from a two-year certificate program or a four-year bachelor's degree program and the successful completion of a licensing examination given by the National Board of Dental Examiners are required to become a registered dental hygienist.

• **The Need.** Employment is expected to grow much faster than the average for all occupations through 2012, in response to increasing demand for dental care and the greater utilization of hygienists to perform services previously performed by dentists. Job prospects are expected to remain excellent. Dental hygienist is expected to be one of the fastest-growing occupations through the year 2012.

• **Number in the Field.** 156,000

• **Salaries.** The average yearly income for beginning dental hygienists is $25,000 to $30,000. More experienced hygienists will earn between $37,000 and $42,000 per year.

For further information write:

American Dental Hygienists' Association
444 North Michigan Avenue, Suite 3400
Chicago, IL 60611
adha.org

Dentist

Dentists examine teeth, oral cavities, and associated tissues. They diagnose and treat disease in these areas, restore defective teeth and tissue, provide aesthetic improvement, reconstruct teeth and oral tissues, and correct facial and dental deformities. New technological areas in dentistry include lasers, cloning, digital imaging, bonding, implants, and electric orthodontics. Dentists also work with government and community groups in maintaining the dental health of the public.

The majority of dentists are self-employed in a private practice. Others specialize as endodontists, oral and maxillofacial surgeons, oral pathologists, orthodontists, periodontists, pediatric dentists, prosthodontists, public health dentists, researchers, and educators.

- **Educational Requirements.** A four-year college or university degree and scoring competitively on the entrance exam for a college of dentistry are required. Upon completing the program, participants are awarded a Doctor of Dental Surgery (D.D.S.) or Doctor of Dental Medicine (D.D.M.). Dentists must also pass the state board examination to practice in most states. Advanced training is required for the dental specialties.
- **The Need.** Employment of dentists is expected to grow more slowly than the average for all occupations through 2012. Although employment growth will provide some job opportunities, most jobs will result from the need to replace the large number of dentists projected to retire. Job prospects should be good as new dentists take over established practices or start their own. However, demand for dental care should grow substantially through 2012, as members of the baby-boom generation advance into middle age.
- **Number in the Field.** 155,000
- **Salaries.** The average salary for a dentist in solo practice was $92,000 annually, while the mean net income of dental specialists was approximately $180,000 annually.

For further information write:

American Dental Association Council on Dental Education
211 East Chicago Avenue
Chicago, IL 60611
ada.org

Medical Assistant

A medical assistant is a person who assists a physician in delivering patient care, most often in the doctor's office. These persons perform a variety of functions such as scheduling appointments; taking blood pressure, respiration, temperature, and other routine patient pre-examination procedures; and performing office and clerical tasks.

A career in medical assistance has the advantage of a short (one- to two-year) post–high school training program. Positions are found in all areas and settings of the country. This career is good for either a recent high school graduate or a person reentering the work force later in life. Medical assistants work in hospitals, clinics, and private physician offices.

- **Educational Requirements.** Graduation from high school with coursework in biology, physical science, secretarial studies, communications, and human relations are necessary. Also, attendance at a one- or two-year accredited medical assisting program is required for certification.
- **The Need.** Medical assistants' positions are expected to grow much faster than the average for all occupations through the year 2012. Increasing utilization of medical assistants in the rapidly growing health care industries will result in fast employment growth for the occupation. In fact, medical assistants are projected to be the fastest growing occupation between 2002 and 2012.
- **Number in the Field.** 278,000
- **Salaries.** For a certified medical assistant with five years' experience, $36,000 a year could be expected.

For further information write:

American Association of Medical Assistants (AAMA)
20 North Wacker Drive, Suite 1575
Chicago, IL 60606
aama-ntl.org

Operating Room Technician

Operating room technicians, sometimes known as surgical technicians, work as part of the surgical team. They assist doctors, nurses, and any operating room workers. Operating room technicians clean and set up the operating room along with prepping and transporting patients to and from the operating room.

- **Educational Requirements.** A high school diploma is required. Most technicians are trained in vocational and technical schools, hospitals, and community colleges. High school courses in health and science are helpful.
- **The Need.** Employment of surgical technologists is expected to grow faster than the average for all occupations through the year 2012 as the volume of surgery increases. Hospitals will continue to be the primary employer of surgical technologists; much faster employment growth is expected in offices of physicians and in outpatient care centers, including ambulatory surgical centers.
- **Number in the Field.** 10,500 to 11,300
- **Salaries.** The average salary is $25,000 to $29,000 a year.

For further information write:

Association for Surgical Technologists
7108 South Alton Way, Building C
Centennial, CO 80112
ast.org

Optometrist

An optometrist is an individual qualified through special training to give visual examinations and other visual services. Optometrists diagnose problems with vision. The optometrist is trained to fit contact lenses or prescription lenses and to detect diseases of the eye. Those interested in pursuing a career as an optometrist should have good vision, mechanical aptitude, and the ability to use delicate precision instruments and be accurate in detailed work.

The majority of optometrists are self-employed. Others work for commercial establishments, in industry, or in teaching or research positions. Some optometrists specialize, for example, in working with children or partially sighted people.

• **Educational Requirements.** A minimum of two years of work at an accredited college in a pre-optometry program is required to enter an optometry college. Training at the optometry school lasts four years, and upon graduation the individual is awarded the Doctor of Optometry degree. To practice, optometrists must pass a written national examination, which is given in segments over the second, third, and fourth year of optometry school. To practice in individual states, an optometrist must also pass a state examination. Some states will accept the national examination as part of the state exam, but all states require some type of oral or practical testing. For research or teaching positions, a graduate degree is necessary.

• **The Need.** Present opportunities for employment are excellent for optometrists who work in private practice and for those employed by large retail optometry firms.

• **Number in the Field.** 29,000

• **Salaries.** The average income for optometrists is approximately $84,000 per year.

For further information write:

American Optometric Association
243 North Lindberg Boulevard
St. Louis, MO 63141
aoanet.org

Osteopathic Physician

Osteopathic physicians and surgeons use currently accepted methods of diagnosing and treating disease and practice all branches of medicine and surgery as M.D.s do; however, they are different in that they emphasize the importance of the musculoskeletal system, holistic medicine, proper nutrition, and environmental factors in maintaining good health. They bring a hands-on approach to medicine and view manipulation or palpation as an aid to the diagnosis and treatment of illness. High scholastic performance, integrity, initiative, an inquiring mind, sound judgment, and emotional stability are necessary.

Osteopathic physicians work primarily in solo private practice, though a growing number are joining group practices. The majority of D.O.s (Doctor of Osteopathy) are general practitioners. They also work in hospitals, research, teaching, military service, medical administration, the government, and public health.

• **Educational Requirements.** A minimum of three years of college or a bachelor's degree and scoring competitively on the Medical College Admission Test (MCAT) are required for entrance into one of the 14 colleges of osteopathic medicine. The majority of these schools offer a four-year program with a few offering the accelerated three-year program. After completion of the program, a Doctor of Osteopathy degree is awarded and a 12-month internship is then required. To further specialize, additional residencies are required, which last from two to six years.

• **The Need.** Osteopathic medicine is geared primarily to the field of general practice. Presently there are many opportunities for general practitioners.

• **Number in the Field.** 52,000

• **Salaries.** The salary of the osteopathic physician is comparable to that of the physician with a medical degree, and the average net income per year is $125,000.

For further information write:

American Osteopathic Association
142 East Ontario Street
Chicago, IL 60611
osteopathic.org

Physician

A physician is a professional who has been trained to care for the health and well being of his or her fellow human beings. The care is preventive or restorative in nature and may be centered on the whole person, as in a general practitioner, or specific parts of the body (specialist), as in the case of a cardiologist. There are many subfields of medicine in which a physician can specialize after completing his or her general training. A person who desires to be a physician should have emotional stability, intelligence, sound judgment, ability to make difficult decisions, good interpersonal skills, and compassion for others.

The majority of physicians are self-employed, but some work in institutional medicine, research or technology, administration, government agencies, public health, or the military.

- **Educational Requirements.** Three or four years of college with courses in biology, chemistry, and other sciences and scoring competitively on the Medical College Admissions Test (MCAT) are needed to gain admission to an accredited college of medicine. Depending upon the curriculum, three or four years of study in medical school, in most cases followed by at least one year as a resident in a postgraduate-based program, are required. To specialize in other areas of medicine, one to six years of postgraduate education may be taken in the postgraduate area of specialization.
- **The Need.** Presently there is a need for family or general practice physicians.
- **Number in the Field.** There are 853,187 M.D. physicians and 50,776 D.O. physicians.
- **Salaries.** Physicians' salaries vary greatly. The annual salary for a physician in family practice is $147,290, in radiology $339,348, and in anesthesiology/surgery $303,341.

For further information write:

American Medical Association
515 North State Street
Chicago, IL 60610
ama-assn.org

Physician Assistant (PA)

The physician assistant is a member of the health care team who is qualified, through academic and clinical training, to provide direct patient care under the instruction and supervision of a licensed physician. The supervising physician is responsible for the physician assistant's performance. The physician assistant assists the physician in medical activities, providing a variety of patient care services, thus giving the physician more time to diagnose and treat patients. These tasks are delegated to the physician assistant within legal parameters and include taking a patient's history, giving physical examinations, performing diagnostic and therapeutic procedures, providing follow-up care, and teaching and counseling the patient. Intelligence, a desire to work with people, emotional maturity, and good communication skills are required for this career.

Physician assistants practice in a variety of settings: private practice (including solo practice) in hospitals, satellite clinics, the armed forces, nursing homes, student health services, government and community agencies, and teaching in physician assistant programs. Physician assistants often act as first or second assistant in major surgery.

- **Educational Requirements.** Training for physician assistants occurs in 56 programs throughout the country. These programs are located in medical schools, public health, allied health school settings, and junior colleges. The programs are two years in length, with the first year consisting of training in the basic medical sciences followed by a second year of clinical experience. Upon graduation the physician assistant is eligible to take a national credentialing examination to become certified. The physician assistant then maintains certification by earning 100 hours of continuing medical education every two years. Recertification through examination is required every six years.
- **The Need.** Currently there are eight opening positions available for every physician assistant graduate. Reimbursement by the government and third-party payors for service rendered by physician assistants has greatly increased the demand.
- **Number in the Field.** 46,000
- **Salaries.** The average income for physician assistants is $64,000.

For further information write:

American Academy of Physician Assistants
950 North Washington Street
Alexandria, VA 22314
aapa.org

Podiatrist

Podiatry is the branch of medicine having to do with the care and treatment of the foot and ankle as its primary focus. Doctors of podiatric medicine diagnose and treat ailments of the feet through medical and surgical means. As the foot often shows the first signs of a general body disorder, the podiatrist also works in detecting diseases like diabetes, ulcers, arthritis, and kidney disorders. An interest in people, deft hands, and an ability for mechanical work are important in this career.

Podiatrists practice in a number of settings: hospitals, special clinics, research, industry, or private practice.

• **Educational Requirements.** Most students have a baccalaureate degree before entering one of the country's five schools of podiatric medicine. After completion of the program, the graduate is awarded the Doctor of Podiatric Medicine degree and is eligible to take the state board examinations. Residencies are also available and are from one to three years in length.

• **The Need.** There is an increasing demand for podiatrists, as foot disorders are among the most widespread and neglected health problems in the country today. In addition, there are a growing number of injuries among men and women who engage in exercise and fitness.

• **Number in the Field.** 17,825

• **Salaries.** Salaries are quite variable depending upon the type of employment. Podiatrists in private practice could earn more than $100,000 annually. Average salary is $80,000.

For further information write:

American Podiatry Medical Association
9312 Old Georgetown Road
Bethesda, MD 20814
apma.org

Psychologist

Psychology is the study of human behavior. A psychologist seeks to understand the aspects of human behavior, including thinking, feeling, development, motivation, perception, learning, the physiological basis of behavior, psychopathology, the relationships of an individual to others, and the environment. Through counseling, individually or in groups, a psychologist works with people to arrive at understanding or insight into their behavior. There are many areas of specialization in the field, some of which are counseling, research, and school, clinical, and social psychology.

Psychologists are employed in a variety of settings, including colleges and universities, business and industry, schools, government, hospitals and rehabilitation centers, the military, and private practice.

• **Educational Requirements.** For licensing as a professional psychologist, most states require a Ph.D. degree from an accredited college or university. A few states permit independent practice with a master's degree.

- **The Need.** Overall employment of psychologists is expected to grow faster than the average for all occupations through 2012, due to increased demand for psychological services in schools, hospitals, social service agencies, mental health centers, substance abuse treatment clinics, consulting firms, and private companies. Demand should be particularly strong for persons holding doctorates from leading universities in applied specialties, such as counseling, health, and school psychology.
- **Number in the Field.** 162,000
- **Salaries.** Starting salaries average between $36,000 and $45,000 a year. Salaries for experienced psychologists average between $60,000 and $95,000 a year.

For further information write:

American Psychological Association
750 First Street NE
Washington, DC 20002
apa.org

4

NURSING

THE FIELD OF nursing plays a key role in providing services to the sick and injured. It also constitutes a major component of the health education system in our country. A variety of challenging opportunities for both men and women are available under the broad category of nursing. Many of the specialties of nursing require an understanding of the patient's social and psychological needs as well as an understanding of the complex science of nursing, which includes knowledge of drugs, treatments, and high-technology equipment.

Within nursing there are separate specialties of nurses. The most common is the registered nurse (R.N.), sometimes referred to as a registered professional nurse. There are more than 2,033,000 R.N.s with 1,627,035 currently employed. There are also about 850,000 practical nurses called L.G.P.N.s or L.P.N.s and many lesser-trained nursing occupations, including nursing aides and orderlies. Some experts estimate that over 50 percent of all the openings in the health care profession in the next decade will occur in nursing.

Some of the specialties in the registered nurse area include the nurse anesthetist, who receives special training to administer anesthesia to patients undergoing surgery. These nurses work under the direct supervision of a physician anesthesiologist and frequently are employed by hospitals or occasionally in private ambulatory clinics and surgical clinics. Many nurses are independent practitioners very much like nurse-midwives, who are registered nurses and qualified by their training and experience to provide obstetrical care to mothers expecting normal delivery. There is a growing interest in the whole area of nurse practitioners. These are registered nurses who have completed a specialty program, usually in one of the medical disciplines, allowing them to perform tasks that historically have been performed by physicians. Frequently they work alongside physicians or occasionally independently in offices, such as hospital outpatient clinics or schools.

The licensed practical nurse (L.P.N.) is a very common occupation, especially in hospitals. More and more as the years have gone by, the licensed practical nurse has taken up much of the bedside care given to hospital patients. They work alongside nursing aides, orderlies, and other nursing assistants who do more of the routine tasks necessary in taking care of patients in a hospital, such as feeding and assisting in bathing the patients. This category of nursing aides, orderlies, and attendants account for the single largest group of employees in the nursing occupation.

Following are a variety of job descriptions and a description of the training necessary for many of the common nursing professions and occupations under the general umbrella of nursing.

Home Health Aide-Homemaker

Nursing, psychiatric, and home health aides-homemakers provide personal and homemaking services to ill, elderly, or disabled persons and to families unable to perform basic tasks for themselves. They provide housekeeping assistance and aid in the care of the patient by performing minor medical treatments. In addition, aides provide patients and their families with instruction and emotional support. The services of a home health aide-homemaker make it possible for an ill, elderly, or disabled person to remain at home rather than in an institution.

- **Educational Requirements.** There are no educational requirements; however, the person who wants to enter this field must have a helpful, compassionate nature, as well as some homemaking knowledge. Some employers have tougher requirements. For admission to a training program, you may require a high school diploma or GED.
- **The Need.** Overall employment of nursing, psychiatric, and home health aides is projected to grow faster than the average for all occupations through the year 2012, although individual occupational growth rates will vary. Employment of home health aides is expected to grow the fastest. Nursing aide employment will not grow as fast as home health aide employment. Employment of psychiatric aides is expected to grow about as fast as the average for all occupations. The number of jobs for psychiatric aides in hospitals, where half of those in the occupation work, will grow slower than the average. Employment in other sectors will rise.
- **Number in the Field.** 415,000
- **Salaries.** Salaries will average $20,000 to $25,000 per year.

For further information write:

National Association for Home Care
228 Seventh Street SE
Washington, DC 20003
nahc.org

Nurse Anesthetist

A nurse anesthetist is a registered professional nurse who has been trained in the administration of anesthesia. The nurse anesthetist may also assist patients with respiratory and cardiopulmonary conditions. After finishing the education and becoming certified, the individual may use the initials C.R.N.A. (Certified Registered Nurse Anesthetist) after his or her name. Today over 50 percent of all anesthesia is administered by nurse anesthetists, under the supervision of an anesthesiologist. Nurse anesthetists should have the ability to make decisions and work under stress, possess emotional stability, and have the ability to work with people.

About 75 percent of all C.R.N.A.s are employed in hospitals. Others work in group practice or independently contract their services as needed.

• **Educational Requirements.** To qualify for training as a nurse anesthetist, the individual must be a graduate of an accredited school of nursing. The training program for nurse anesthetists takes from 18 to 20 months and is offered in 175 hospitals and university settings. Upon graduation, a diploma is granted and the individual is eligible to sit for the national qualifying examination to gain initial certification. C.R.N.A.s must be recertified every two years by the Council on Recertification of Nurse Anesthetists.

• **The Need.** There is a need for C.R.N.A.s today. The outlook is good, particularly in those hospitals in rural areas and in some large cities.

• **Number in the Field.** 26,000

• **Salaries.** The starting salary for a nurse anesthetist is approximately $56,000 per year. Experienced C.R.N.A.s can earn a mean salary of $70,000 to $75,000.

For further information write:

American Association of Nurse Anesthetists
222 South Prospect Avenue
Park Ridge, IL 60068
aana.com

Licensed Practical Nurse (L.P.N.)

A licensed graduate practical nurse provides nursing care to the sick. Nursing duties involve taking and recording temperatures, blood pressure, pulse, and respiration rates. They may administer medications under supervision. Other duties are dressing wounds; applying compresses, ice bags, and hot water bottles; and giving alcohol rubs and massages. The practical nurse assists the professional nurse and/or physician by observing the patient and reporting any changes in his or her condition. A person interested in being a licensed practical nurse should be friendly, compassionate, warm, sympathetic, emotionally stable, and have the ability to work with all types of people.

Licensed practical nurses work in hospitals, nursing homes, clinics, physicians' offices, and industrial medicine. Recently there has been a shift in employment opportunities from the acute-care setting to the long-term care setting.

• **Educational Requirements.** Training to become a licensed practical nurse involves one year in an approved school of practical nursing. Upon completion of training, students must pass a state board examination to become licensed.

• **The Need.** At present, the demand exceeds the number of nurses available, making opportunities in nursing excellent. The need for L.P.N.s in rural areas is extensive.

- **Number in the Field.** 1,000,000
- **Salaries.** The average salary for a licensed practical nurse ranges from $27,000 to $32,000.

For further information write:

National Federation of Licensed Practical Nurses
605 Poole Drive
Gamer, NC 27529
nflpn.org

Nurse-Midwife

A nurse-midwife is a person who practices the independent management and care of normal newborns and women. This individual has been educated in the disciplines of nursing and midwifery and is certified by the American College of Nurse-Midwives. The nurse-midwife provides care and emotional support for the mother during pregnancy and supervises and evaluates the progress of labor. After delivery, the midwife evaluates and provides care for the newborn. He or she also assists the mother with breast and bottle-feeding and self-care and teaches the mother about the infant's development. Nurse-midwives need to be able to work in stressful situations and have good communication skills and above average intelligence.

Nurse-midwives work in hospitals, health maintenance organizations, family planning centers, public health services, alternative birth centers, private practices, and birthing centers.

- **Educational Requirements.** Training for a nurse-midwife is offered as a post-R.N. program or at the master's degree level. The post-R.N. program offers courses on theory and clinical experience. The degree program offers courses in nurse-midwifery leading to a master's degree. Upon graduation the person is eligible to take the American College of Nurse-Midwives national examination for certification.

• **The Need.** Presently, nurse-midwives have few problems finding employment. The employment outlook is projected to be good through the year 2012.

• **Number in the Field.** 5,000

• **Salaries.** The starting salary for a nurse-midwife ranges from $60,000 to $100,000 a year.

For further information write:

American College of Nurse-Midwives
818 Connecticut Avenue NW, Suite 900
Washington, DC 20005
acnm.org

Nurse Practitioner (N.P.)

A nurse practitioner is an R.N. who is functioning in an expanded nursing role, usually in an ambulatory patient care setting. In most cases he or she works closely with a physician. However, a few have established independent practices. This position requires graduation from any level nursing program and an additional four months to one year of apprenticeship or formal training to become a pediatric nurse practitioner, obstetrical nurse practitioner (midwife), or family nurse practitioner.

The nurse practitioner is contrasted with the clinical nurse specialist, who functions as a partner with the physician rather than in a subservient role. The clinical nurse specialist must have a master's degree with education in such specialties as pediatrics, obstetrics, or psychiatry.

The nurse clinician is another extension of the R.N. It is a middle-level position of nursing practice that is attained by demonstrating advanced clinical competence in providing leadership for the nursing team. She or he may be prepared at the diploma, bachelor's, or master's level.

- **Educational Requirements.** A nurse practitioner can be a graduate of any level nursing program plus four months to one year of apprenticeship or formal training in pediatrics, obstetrics, or psychiatry. A clinical nurse specialist must obtain a master's degree with education in such specialties as pediatrics or obstetrics. A nurse clinician can be a graduate of any level nursing program.
- **The Need.** The outlook is bright both in hospitals and with outpatient group practices and individual physicians.
- **Number in the Field.** 20,000
- **Salaries.** The average starting salary is approximately $35,000, and the average maximum salary is between $47,000 and $57,000.

For further information write:

American Nurses Association
600 Maryland Avenue SW
Washington, DC 20024-2571
nursingworld.org

Registered Nurse (R.N.)

The registered nurse is a professional who is responsible for planning, giving, and supervising the bedside nursing care of patients. He or she also instructs nursing personnel and gives teaching programs to patients and their families. Working in an administrative capacity, a registered nurse can assist in daily operations, oversee various programs in hospital or institutional settings, or plan for the delivery of community health services. A person who desires a career as a registered nurse should have an ability to work with people; be understanding and compassionate; have the administrative abilities of planning, coordinating, and decision making; and have emotional stability.

Registered nurses work in a variety of settings: hospitals, nursing homes, public health agencies, industry, physician offices, government agencies, and educational settings.

- **Educational Requirements.** Training to become a registered nurse can be done in several ways. It can be a two-year associate's degree program, a two- or three-year diploma program, a four-year baccalaureate program, or master's degree programs that have a clinical specialty. For licensure, graduates must pass a state board examination. A master's or doctorate degree is required to work in a supervisory, administrative, teaching, or research capacity. These programs are offered at colleges and universities.
- **The Need.** Presently the demand for inpatient nurses has leveled off.
- **Number in the Field.** 2,300,000
- **Salaries.** The average starting salary for a staff registered nurse is $30,000 and the average maximum salary is $40,000.

For further information write:

American Nurses Association
600 Maryland Avenue SW
Washington, DC 20024-2571
nursingworld.org

Nursing Aide/Psychiatric Aide and Orderly

A nursing aide is a person who assists in the direct care of a patient under the supervision of the nursing staff. Typical functions include making beds, bathing patients, taking vital signs, serving food trays, and transporting a patient to and from treatment areas. Aides should be sensitive to the physical needs of patients and enjoy working with people.

Nursing aides are employed in psychiatric and acute-care hospitals, nursing homes, and home health agencies.

- **Educational Requirements.** Nursing aides are trained in a number of settings: vocational/technical programs, high school programs, or in a hospital or nursing home. The training program consists of lectures, demonstrations, and supervised practice.
- **The Need.** Presently the demand for nursing aides exceeds the supply, producing excellent employment opportunities.
- **Number in the Field.** 1,300,000 (including orderlies) and 100,000 psychiatric aides
- **Salaries.** The average annual salary for a nursing assistant is $16,500.

For further information contact the personnel department of your neighborhood hospital or nursing home.

5

Therapists on the Medical Team

The main role of the therapist on the medical team is to help patients recover from their injuries, illnesses, and handicaps. Therapists attempt to bring the patient to that level of self-help and independence to function as close to normal as possible.

There are many different types of therapists, with each type having its own skills, talents, and specialized knowledge. Some of the common traits cross the therapists' ranks for all therapist disciplines, namely the skills of a concerned teacher. This is tremendously important in dealing with patients in therapy.

Physical therapists work with patients' muscular and skeletal structures. They use exercise extensively and the therapeutic application of heat, cold, and electricity. Occupational therapists are concerned with aiding and improving the patient's daily living and job skills, frequently using manual and industrial arts to rehabilitate their patients.

Some of the newer forms of therapy include dance and art techniques, which have been found useful as a nonverbal means of communication and have proven helpful in aiding patients to resolve emotional and social problems. The field of therapy now embraces the use of gardening for the purpose of training handicapped patients and evaluating their abilities. These specialists are called horticultural therapists.

The area of therapy and its related activities is quite broad and offers to interested individuals a wide range of specializations requiring different skills, interests, and knowledge.

AIDS Counselor

AIDS counselors provide support and help for those suffering from AIDS (Acquired Immune Deficiency Syndrome). AIDS counselors offer instructions for AIDS prevention to high-risk groups and information to the public. AIDS counselors assist those who are about to be tested for HIV.

- **Educational Requirements.** There is no formal training for AIDS counselors. The best way to become a counselor is to be a volunteer first.
- **The Need.** The outlook for paid employment is uncertain. The demand for volunteers will remain high; however, paid positions will depend on the level of funding. Opportunities for those with master's degrees and experience in a related field will be abundant.
- **Number in the Field.** 2,000 to 3,500 working in the health care industry
- **Salaries.** Salaries vary, but those in paid positions with a bachelor's degree earn about $30,000 per year, and those with a master's degree earn $40,000 per year.

For further information write:

The Academy for Educational Development
1825 Connecticut Avenue NW
Washington, DC 20037
aed.org

Art Therapist

Art therapy is used to provide the patient with an opportunity for nonverbal expression through works of art. The creative process that occurs in art enables the patient to resolve emotional conflicts and develop a sense of awareness and personal growth. The art therapist assists the patient by art instruction and positive reinforcement. The therapeutic process enables a patient to establish a better and more meaningful relationship with the world. Sensitivity to human needs, patience, and the ability to work with the mentally and emotionally handicapped are necessary in this field.

Art therapists practice in many settings: hospitals, rehabilitation centers, psychiatric hospitals, and in community mental health workshops.

- **Educational Requirements.** A bachelor's degree with a major in art is needed to enter the field. To practice on the professional level requires a master's degree or its equivalent in training. Students should look for programs that offer instruction in the dual areas of the fine arts and the behavioral and social sciences.
- **The Need.** Art therapy is a growing field.
- **Number in the Field.** 3,850
- **Salaries.** Annual salaries for art therapists range from $30,000 to $42,000 depending upon education, experience, and the type of

institution. Art therapists who work in private practice establish their own fees.

For further information write:

American Art Therapy Association
1202 Allanson Road
Mundelein, IL 60060
arttherapy.org

Audiologist and Speech Therapist

An audiologist is a professional who specializes in the identification and prevention of hearing problems and in nonmedical rehabilitation of these problems. The audiologist assesses an individual to determine if a hearing impairment exists, evaluates the nature and extent of the problem, and determines whether a hearing aid might be beneficial in treating the problem. Patience and perseverance are needed in this profession, as speech and hearing rehabilitation is a slow process.

Audiologists practice in hospitals, schools, rehabilitation centers, colleges and universities, state and federal government, and they also work independently in private practice.

Speech-language pathologists, sometimes called speech therapists, assess, diagnose, treat, and help to prevent speech, language, cognitive, communication, voice, swallowing, fluency, and other related disorders. Specifically they work with:

- People who cannot make speech sounds, or cannot make them clearly.
- People with speech rhythm and fluency problems, such as stuttering.

- People with voice quality problems, such as inappropriate pitch or harsh voice.
- People with problems understanding and producing language.
- People who wish to improve their communication skills by modifying an accent.
- People with cognitive communication impairments, such as attention, memory, and problem-solving disorders.
- People with hearing loss who use hearing aids or cochlear implants to develop auditory skills and improve communication.

Most speech-language pathologists provide direct clinical services to individuals with communication or swallowing disorders. Some speech-language pathologists conduct research on how people communicate. Others design and develop equipment or techniques for diagnosing and treating speech problems.

- **Educational Requirements.** To practice, an audiologist must have successfully completed a two-year master's degree program and passed a national examination given by the American-Speech-Language-Hearing Association. Doctoral degrees are also granted.
- **The Need.** Employment is expected to grow faster than the average for all occupations through the year 2012. Employment in educational services will increase along with growth in elementary and secondary school enrollments, including enrollment of special education students. Federal law guarantees special education and related services to all eligible children with disabilities. The number of speech-language pathologists in private practice will rise due to the increasing use of contract services by hospitals, schools, and nursing care facilities.

- **Number in the Field.** 9,200 certified audiologists and 1,750 certified audiologists/speech pathologists
- **Salaries.** Starting salary averages $28,000 to $34,000 a year. The average salary is $36,000 to $50,000 a year.

For further information write:

American Speech-Language-Hearing Association
10801 Rockville Pike
Rockville, MD 20852
asha.org

Dance Therapist

A dance therapist works with persons with learning, behavioral, perceptual, and physical disorders. He or she assists in the development of the emotional and physical integration of a patient through the use of dance movement. A dance therapist should display emotional maturity, patience, and physical stamina.

Dance therapists work in hospitals, psychiatric hospitals, community mental health centers, health care facilities, special schools, rehabilitation facilities, and correctional facilities. They also are involved in consulting and research.

- **Educational Requirements.** A bachelor's degree with courses in dance movement, psychology, and a master's degree in dance therapy from an American Dance Therapy Association–approved program are required for registry.
- **The Need.** Opportunities are expected to increase provided there is federal support for mental health.
- **Number in the Field.** 850

- **Salaries.** Depending upon education, experience, and abilities, salaries for dance therapists range from $25,000 to $50,000.

For further information write:

American Dance Therapy Association
2000 Century Plaza, Suite 230
Columbia, MD 21044
adta.org

Dietitian

A dietitian, sometimes called a nutritionist, assists patients and their families in choosing foods for adequate nutrition throughout the life cycle. Dietitians also assist the food service director in the preparation and serving of food to groups, participate in research, and teach classes in nutrition. The ability to organize work and supervise people, an analytical mind, and good communication skills are important in this position.

Dietitians work in community health agencies, hospitals, clinics, and other health facilities; in consultation or private practice; in management practices; and as teachers in colleges and universities.

- **Educational Requirements.** Four years of specialized study at a college or university followed by a postgraduate dietetic internship are required. A national examination given by the American Dietetic Association is needed for registration.
- **The Need.** Employment of dietitians is expected to grow about as fast as the average for all occupations through 2012. The number of dietitian positions in nursing care facilities and in state government is expected to decline slightly. Employment is

expected to grow rapidly in contract providers of food services, outpatient care centers, and offices of physicians and other health practitioners.

- **Number in the Field.** 62,000
- **Salaries.** The average salary for dietitians with one to five years of experience is $30,000 to $42,000 per year. More experienced dietitians earn $42,000 to $50,000 per year.

For further information write:

American Dietetic Association
216 West Jackson Boulevard
Chicago, IL 60606
eatright.org

Horticultural Therapist

Horticultural therapists use gardening activities and plants to affect a positive change in the social, educational, psychological, and physical adjustment of people. They work with people who are physically disabled, ill, developmentally disabled, mentally ill, elderly, public offenders, and socially disadvantaged. Horticultural therapy aims to improve attitudes through a change in self-concept.

Horticultural therapists work in public or private facilities for the handicapped, including convalescent homes, juvenile centers, schools and training centers for the mentally retarded, psychiatric hospitals, and general care hospitals.

- **Educational Requirements.** A bachelor's degree in horticultural therapy is required, and there are graduate programs available as well.

• **The Need.** Horticultural therapy is becoming more recognized as a valuable resource in rehabilitation therapy and, therefore, employment opportunities are growing.
   • **Number in the Field.** 2,200
   • **Salaries.** Salaries range from $18,000 to $28,000.

For further information write:

The American Horticultural Therapy Association
909 York Street
Denver, CO 80206
ahta.org

Hospice Worker

Hospice workers care for people who are terminally ill. They also help families adjust to the loss of a loved one. Hospice workers include nurses, doctors, counselors, social workers, clergy, and homemakers and health aides. They work together to make sure that the patient's needs are met and that family members receive support.

   • **Educational Requirements.** Specialized training is given to hospice workers.
   • **The Need.** Uncertain.
   • **Number in the Field.** 3,500 to 5,000
   • **Salaries.** Many hospice workers are volunteers and receive no salary. Most, however, receive the same earnings as a hospital counterpart.

For further information write:

National Hospice and Palliative Care Organization
1700 Diagonal Road, Suite 625
Alexandria, VA 22314
nhpco.org

Hospital Chaplain

The hospital chaplain provides the patients and members of the family with pastoral care and religious counseling. The chaplain visits newly admitted patients and assists with their adjustment to the hospital, makes routine visits to rooms and wards, and performs church rites or makes provisions with an appropriate religious leader to do so. The chaplain contacts the patient's religious leader and informs him/her of the hospitalization and condition of the patient. The chaplain leads chapel functions and acts as a liaison between hospital staff and the patient's family and friends during a time of crisis. Educational planning and programming for the in-service training of pastoral students and religious professionals may also be a part of the responsibilities. The chaplain assists local clergy in rendering pastoral care and is an important part of the total patient care program. Persons intending to pursue a career in hospital ministry should have a genuine concern for people, good communication skills, compassion, and emotional stability.

- **Educational Requirements.** A bachelor's degree and a degree from a theological seminary are the basic entrance requirements for the field. An internship in clinical pastoral education and advanced degrees in pastoral psychology are the additional training requirements.
- **The Need.** There appears to be a growing need for hospital chaplains and for those working in long-term care institutions.

• **Salaries.** Salaries range from $36,000 to $48,000. Salaries will vary depending upon the type of religious order and the amount of education and experience.

For further information contact a hospital that offers accredited chaplaincy training programs.

Music Therapist

A music therapist works with victims of hearing loss and blindness, the mentally retarded, and the emotionally disturbed in planning and directing medically prescribed musical activities with the goal of improving their outlook and assisting in their rehabilitation. Considering the needs of the patient, the therapist works in collaboration with physicians and other members of the patient care team in planning a course of treatment. Therapy for the patient includes listening and participating in solo and group musical activities. Goals of therapy include increased self-confidence, better self-control, longer attention span, and relief from chronic depression or anger. Persons entering this field should be serious musicians with good communication skills and have a preference for working with people to improve their social adjustment.

Musical therapists work in hospitals, schools, mental health agencies, retirement homes, government, and community health agencies.

• **Educational Requirements.** To enter the field, a bachelor's degree in music therapy from a college or university program approved by the National Association for Music Therapy or the American Association for Music Therapy, and a six-month internship at an approved institution are required. After receiving the bachelor's degree and completing the internship, the individual is eligible for certification.

• **The Need.** The field of music therapy is growing and offers good employment and advancement opportunities for qualified individuals.

• **Number in the Field.** 4,000

• **Salaries.** Salaries for music therapists vary between $26,000 and $39,000.

For further information write:

American Association for Music Therapy
8455 Colesville Road, Suite 1000
Silver Spring, MD 20910
musictherapy.org

Occupational Therapist

Occupational therapists are concerned with persons who have experienced physical injuries or illnesses, psychological or developmental problems, or problems associated with the aging process. The therapist coordinates a variety of educational, vocational, and rehabilitation therapies to allow the patient to become as self-sufficient as possible and lead a normal life in work, education, and pleasure. Tact, creativity, ability to solve complex living problems, and an interest in helping others are necessary. Occupational therapists work in hospitals, clinics, extended-care facilities, rehabilitation hospitals, government agencies, and community agencies.

• **Educational Requirements.** Four years of college with a major in occupational therapy is the training required to become an occupational therapist. A master's degree or a certificate program can be completed for those individuals who already have a bachelor's degree. Upon graduation, a national certification examination must be taken to become a registered occupational therapist.

- **The Need.** There is a current need for registered occupational therapists.
- **Number in the Field.** 52,000
- **Salaries.** Starting salaries average between $30,000 and $38,000 a year. Salaries for experienced occupational therapists average between $39,000 and $50,000 a year.

For further information write:

The American Occupational Therapy Association
4720 Montgomery Lane
P.O. Box 31220
Bethesda, MD 20824-1220
aota.org

Occupational Therapy Assistant

An occupational therapy assistant helps conduct a series of educational, vocational, and rehabilitation activities aimed at helping disabled or injured individuals to reach their highest functional levels possible. This individual works under the supervision of an occupational therapist and assists by preparing materials for activities, maintaining tools and equipment, and recording and reporting on a patient's progress. Those seeking employment as occupational therapy assistants should have a desire to help others and display understanding, tact, and patience when working with the disabled. Occupational therapy assistants work in hospitals, nursing homes, rehabilitation centers, psychiatric hospitals, and military and veterans hospitals.

- **Educational Requirements.** Preparation for a career as an occupational therapy assistant can be done at a two-year associate's degree program or a one-year program at an accredited institution or through a 25-week program conducted in a hospital setting.
- **The Need.** The employment outlook for occupational therapy assistants is very good.
- **Number in the Field.** 10,500
- **Salaries.** The average annual salary for an occupational therapy assistant is $25,000 to $29,000.

For further information write:

The American Occupational Therapy Association
4720 Montgomery Lane
P.O. Box 31220
Bethesda, MD 20824-1220
aota.org

Ophthalmic Technician/Assistant

Ophthalmic technologists and ophthalmic assistants aid ophthalmologists with some of the more routine functions such as simple vision testing, taking medical histories, administering eye drops, and changing dressings. The technician does more advanced work, while the assistant does the more routine tasks. Ophthalmic technicians and ophthalmic assistants work for ophthalmologists in their offices, in clinics, or in hospitals.

• **Educational Requirements.** Ophthalmic technicians and ophthalmic assistants both are required to take an approved institutional course of one year or less. These courses are given at medical schools, colleges, and hospitals. In addition, a year of supervised work experience is required.

• **The Need.** The employment outlook is excellent, as there is a great need for ophthalmic technicians.

• **Number in the Field.** 4,500 ophthalmic assistants and 3,200 ophthalmic technicians

• **Salaries.** The assistant begins at approximately $25,000 to $29,000 a year.

For further information write:

Joint Commission on Allied Health Personnel in Ophthalmology
2025 Woodlane Drive
St. Paul, MN 55125-2998
jcahpo.org

Ophthalmic Technologist

The ophthalmic technologist is a skilled person who assists the ophthalmologist in advanced areas of microbiology, advanced color vision, ophthalmic photography, special instruments and diagnostic techniques, and operating room procedures. Ophthalmic technologists work in ophthalmologists' offices and in specialized eye-care institutions.

• **Educational Requirements.** The applicant for the position of ophthalmic technologist must have completed a four-year college degree program in ophthalmic technology, must be endorsed by the program director, and must possess a nationally recognized certificate of competence in cardiopulmonary resuscitation. There are allowable equivalencies involving a combination of academic work and clinical experience.

• **The Need.** At present employment opportunities are excellent, as there are more positions available than persons to fill them.

• **Number in the Field.** 475 (certified)

• **Salaries.** The starting salary for an ophthalmic technologist is approximately $21,620 to $24,460.

For further information write:

Joint Commission on Allied Health Personnel in Ophthalmology
2025 Woodlane Drive
St. Paul, MN 55125-2998
jcahpo.org

Orthoptist

Orthoptics is a science that deals with ocular mobility, binocular vision, and related disorders of the eyes. An orthoptist is a specialist in the eye muscles and treats deficient eye coordination, movement, and vision while working under the supervision of an ophthalmologist. Many orthoptists work with specialized pediatric ophthalmologists because a large percentage of the patients are children. Persons who desire to work as orthoptists should have good vision and an interest in science. Personal qualities include patience, understanding, sound judgment, and emotional maturity.

Orthoptists work with one or more ophthalmologists in private practice offices, hospitals, or medical schools.

• **Educational Requirements.** An orthoptist must complete a minimum of two years in an accredited college or university, although four years are preferred. Upon completion of training, for certification the individual must pass a written, oral, and practical examination given by the American Orthoptic Council.

• **The Need.** With the increase in alternative health care delivery systems, there is a constant high demand for orthoptists in the workforce.

• **Number in the Field.** 550

• **Salaries.** Salary varies with the type of setting. It can range from $28,000 to $35,000 per year.

For further information write:

American Orthoptic Council
3914 Nakoma Road
Madison, WI 53711
orthoptics.org

Physical Therapist

A physical therapist plans and administers physical therapy treatment programs for medically referred patients to restore function, relieve pain, and prevent disability following disease, injury, or loss of body parts. A physical therapist uses the treatment modalities of electricity, heat, cold, ultrasound, massage, and exercise. He or she also helps the patient in emotionally accepting his/her disability and in encouraging development. Responsibility, sincerity, and emotional stability are assets in seeking a career in physical therapy.

Physical therapists work in hospitals, outpatient clinics, rehabilitation centers, home care agencies, nursing homes, voluntary health agencies, private practices, sports medicine centers, educational systems, and in clinical research activities.

- **Educational Requirements.** A four-year program in physical therapy from an accredited college or university with a specified period of clinical education is required. Certificate programs lasting from 12 to 16 months and master's-level programs are offered for those who already have a college degree. By 1990, all programs were at the graduate level.
- **The Need.** Employment of physical therapists is expected to grow faster than the average for all occupations through 2012. The demand for physical therapists should continue to rise as growth in the number of individuals with disabilities or limited function spurs demand for therapy services. The growing elderly population is particularly vulnerable to chronic and debilitating conditions that require therapeutic services. Also, the baby-boom generation is entering the prime age for heart attacks and strokes, increasing the demand for cardiac and physical rehabilitation. Further, because technological advances save the lives of a larger proportion of newborns with severe birth defects, these young people will need physical therapy, too.
- **Number in the Field.** 100,000+
- **Salaries.** Salaries for recent graduates range from $35,000 to $50,000 a year.

For further information write:

American Physical Therapy Association
1111 North Fairfax Street
Alexandria, VA 22314
apta.org

Physical Therapy Aide

The role of the physical therapy aide is to assist the physical therapist in patient care. The responsibilities include preparing and maintaining treatment areas. Physical therapy aides do not have any direct patient contact. An interest in working with people, the ability to communicate, and a pleasant personality are assets in this position.

Physical therapy aides work in hospitals, rehabilitation centers, nursing homes, military and veterans hospitals, and in psychiatric hospitals.

- **Educational Requirements.** High school graduation or the equivalent is required for this position.
- **The Need.** Most physical therapy aides have completed on-the-job training; therefore, the positions are limited.
- **Salaries.** Salaries may be as high as $20,000 to $25,000 a year.

For further information write:

American Physical Therapy Association
1111 North Fairfax Street
Alexandria, VA 22314
apta.org

Physical Therapy Assistant

A physical therapy assistant works under the direction of a physical therapist and assists in the treatment of the patient. The assistant follows the patient care program devised by the physical therapist and physician by performing tests and treatment procedures, assembling equipment necessary for procedures, and observing and reporting on a patient's behavior. Maturity, patience, and a desire to help people are assets in this position.

Physical therapy assistants practice in hospitals, nursing homes, rehabilitation centers, and community and government agencies, to name some examples.

• **Educational Requirements.** Training for a physical therapy assistant position is a two-year associate's degree program. At present, licensing is required in only a few states.

• **The Need.** There is a need for physical therapy assistants as there are not enough assistants to meet the demand throughout the country.

• **Number in the Field.** 20,000 to 25,000

• **Salaries.** Salaries for recent graduates from a physical therapy assistant program range from $25,000 to $30,000 per year.

For further information write:

American Physical Therapy Association
1111 North Fairfax Street
Alexandria, VA 22314
apta.org

Prosthetist and Orthotist

Prosthetics are surgical or dental devices that are used as an artificial replacement for a missing body part. A prosthetist is a specialist who measures, manufactures, and fits these artificial devices. The specialist also instructs an individual in the use of prosthetics. An orthotist is a specialist who manufactures and fits braces and other orthopedic devices.

Prosthetists and orthotists work in business, hospitals, and rehabilitation centers.

• **Educational Requirements.** There are three ways to pursue this career: First, by obtaining an associate's degree from an accredited college and completing a training program that is certified by the American Board of Certification in Prosthetics and Orthotics, plus four years of experience in the field. Second, by attending a college that offers a bachelor's degree program in prosthetics and orthotics, and one year of experience. Third, by obtaining a bachelor's degree in any subject and completing the training program certified by the American Board of Certification in Prosthetics and Orthotics, and one year of experience.

• **The Need.** There is a shortage of prosthetists and orthotists. Employment opportunities are very good.

• **Number in the Field.** 2,200 certified orthotists, 2,500 certified prosthetists, 1,000 certified orthotists/prosthetists

• **Salaries.** Salaries for those with a bachelor's degree range from $39,000 to $55,000. The average salary for a technician is $28,000 to $35,000 a year.

For further information write:

American Academy of Orthotists and Prosthetists
1650 King Street, Suite 502
Alexandria, VA 22314
oandp.org

Radiation Therapy Technologist

A radiation therapy technologist helps the radiologist in treating afflicted areas of a patient's body with prescribed doses of ionizing radiation. The technologist is responsible for maintaining the radiation treatment equipment in proper operating order and shares responsibility with the radiologist for the accuracy of treatment records. To operate the complex equipment, a radiology technologist should be mechanically inclined and, in addition, have an aptitude for mathematics and the physical sciences.

Radiation therapy technologists work in hospitals, laboratories, clinics, physicians' offices, government agencies, and in industry.

- **Educational Requirements.** There are two educational routes to prepare for a career as a radiation therapy technologist: the one-year and the two-year program. An applicant to an approved one-year educational program must be either a graduate of an approved educational program in radiologic technology, a registered nurse with education in radiation physics, or have equivalent qualifications. The program should be 12 months in length and include courses in physics, math, pathology, radiobiology, anatomy, treatment planning, radium procedures, nursing procedures, protection and shielding, and ethics.

An alternate two-year educational course was approved by the AMA House of Delegates in 1972. Applicants to the program need not be graduates of approved teaching programs in radiologic technology, but they must be high school graduates with course work in science and math. This course teaches principles in the use of ionizing radiation and related basic courses.

- **The Need.** There is a shortage of technicians in the field.
- **Number in the Field.** 6,000 to 7,000
- **Salaries.** Salaries range from $25,000 to $35,000 per year.

For further information write:

American Society of Radiologic Technologists
1500 Central Avenue SE
Albuquerque, NM 87123
asrt.org

American Society of Radiologic Technologies
55 East Jackson Street, Suite 1020
Chicago, IL 60604
asrt.org

Recreational Therapist

A recreational therapist is responsible for directing a program of recreational activities with the aim of assisting in the recovery from or adjustment to an illness, disability, or specific social problem. Recreation therapy is a subdivision of the recreation field. These programs are directed at the ill or disabled and are usually conducted in nonmedical settings such as community recreation agencies. Individuals who seek employment as a recreational therapist should enjoy working with people, be able to transmit enthusiasm, and have imaginative minds and well-developed communication skills. Recreation therapists work in general and psychiatric hospitals, nursing homes, and community centers and recreation agencies.

• **Educational Requirements.** The career field of recreational therapy can be entered at many different levels. A two-year associate's degree in therapeutic recreation allows one to work in positions with limited responsibilities in program design. A bachelor's degree permits professional status and enables an individual to assume a more responsible role. Individuals must complete four hundred hours of clinical training at an approved hospital. A master's degree in recreation therapy prepares one for an executive-level position with responsibilities in the areas of research, teaching, and administration. The states of Georgia and Utah require all recreational therapists to be licensed.

- **The Need.** Recreational therapy is one of the fastest-growing occupations.
- **Number in the Field.** 15,000 (certified) and a total of 40,000 in practice
- **Salaries.** Salary varies with the type of setting. It can range from $30,000 to $50,000.

For further information write:

American Therapeutic Recreation Association
2021 W Street NW, Suite 250
Washington, DC 20036
atra-tr.org

Respiratory Therapist

Respiratory therapy is the diagnostic evaluation, treatment, and care of persons with deficiencies and abnormalities associated with the cardiopulmonary system. Using respiratory equipment, the therapist helps patients with asthma, emphysema, pneumonia, and bronchitis. In treatment, a therapist uses medical gases and various therapeutic modalities to include blood gas acquisition and analysis, inspiratory positive pressure breathing, chest physiotherapy, pulmonary rehabilitation, and mechanical ventilation. Respiratory therapists play an active role in newborn, pediatric, and adult intensive care. The respiratory therapist, under the supervision of a physician, performs these therapeutic procedures based on his or her observation of the patient. Persons aspiring to be a respiratory therapist should have mechanical ability to work the respiratory equipment, a sense of responsibility, compassion, and the ability to work with a variety of people.

Respiratory therapists work in hospitals, nursing homes, physicians' offices, and commercial companies that provide emergency oxygen equipment and services to home-care patients.

- **Educational Requirements.** Training to become a respiratory therapist involves a two-year program leading to an associate's or bachelor's degree. The training consists of classroom education in biology and the physical sciences that are related to the human respiratory system. Clinical training is the second half of the program. Prerequisites to enter the program include courses in biology and in the physical, medical, and social sciences. After graduating from the program, an individual may enter the credentialing process of the National Board for Respiratory Therapy to become a registered respiratory therapist (R.R.T.).
- **The Need.** Job opportunities are expected to be very good. Employment of respiratory therapists is expected to increase faster than the average for all occupations through the year 2012. Although hospitals will continue to employ the vast majority of therapists, a growing number can expect to work outside of hospitals in home health-care services, offices of physicians or other health practitioners, or durable medical equipment firms.
- **Number in the Field.** 156,000 practicing respiratory therapists and technicians.

- **Salaries.** The entry-level salary for a respiratory therapist is $30,000 to $40,000 per year. Experienced respiratory therapists earn from $45,000 to $50,000 per year.

For further information write:

American Association for Respiratory Care
9425 North MacArthur Boulevard, Suite 100
Irving, TX 75063
aarc.org

Respiratory Therapy Technician

Respiratory therapy is the diagnostic evaluation, treatment, and care of persons with deficiencies and abnormalities that are associated with the cardiopulmonary system. The respiratory therapy technician works under the supervision of a physician and a respiratory therapist in administering various types of therapeutic modalities to include medical gases, aerosol therapy and aerosolized medication, intermittent-positive pressure breathing treatments, chest physiotherapy, pulmonary rehabilitation, and both short- and long-term continuous artificial ventilation. Responsibilities also include cleaning, sterilizing, and maintaining the respiratory equipment, and recording the patient's therapy in the medical record. Persons who seek to become respiratory therapy technicians should have mechanical aptitude to operate the respiratory equipment, compassion, and the ability to work with all types of people.

Respiratory therapy technicians work in hospitals, nursing homes, physicians' offices, and commercial companies that provide emergency oxygen equipment and therapeutic modalities to patients in the home.

• **The Need.** Opportunities for employment are good as the demand for manpower has exceeded the supply.

• **Number in the Field.** There are a total of 58,000 practicing respiratory therapists and technicians.

• **Salaries.** The entry-level salary for a respiratory therapy technician is $24,000 to $29,000.

For further information write:

American Association for Respiratory Care
9425 North MacArthur Boulevard, Suite 100
Irving, TX 75063
aarc.org

Social Worker

The social worker helps patients and their families with emotional, social, and environmental problems related to illness or hospitalization. He or she evaluates the patient's family functioning, home environment, and community supports. The social worker works closely with other hospital professionals and community agencies to deal with such problems as adjustment to chronic illness or disability, drug and alcohol addiction, abuse or neglect, problem pregnancies, vocational difficulties, financial problems, rehabilitation or long-term care services, and terminal illness. Social workers may give individual counseling, family treatment, or group work. They are employed in hospitals, health centers, nursing homes, government, and community agencies. Some are involved in industry and labor as well as the judicial system.

- **Educational Requirements.** A bachelor's degree in social work is the minimum requirement for this position. To practice professionally, a master's degree in social work is required.
- **The Need.** The need for social workers is widely recognized and job opportunities are good for those entering the field.
- **Number in the Field.** 125,000
- **Salaries.** The annual beginning salary for a social worker with a bachelor's degree is $25,000, with a master's $35,000, and for those who have been certified by the Academy of Certified Social Workers, the salary is $45,000.

For further information write:

National Association of Social Workers
750 First Street NE, Suite 700
Washington, DC 20002-4241
naswdc.org

Substance Abuse Counselor

Substance abuse counselors are social workers who assist people with problems with alcohol and/or drugs. Counselors instruct addicts and people who are concerned that they may become addicted. The counselors also speak with former addicts and on occasion speak with families of addicts.

- **Educational Requirements.** High school plus training is required.
- **The Need.** Employment of social workers is expected to grow faster than the average for all occupations through 2012. The rapidly growing elderly population and the aging baby-boom gen-

eration will create greater demand for health and social services. Employment of social workers in private social service agencies will increase. Opportunities for social workers in private practice will expand but growth may be somewhat hindered by restrictions that managed care organizations put on mental health services.

- **Number in the Field.** 4,000 to 5,000
- **Salaries.** Starting salary is $20,000 to $29,000, and the average salary for experienced substance abuse counselors is $25,000 to $34,000 per year.

For further information write:

Alcohol and Drug Problem Association of North America
307 North Main
St. Charles, MO 63301
adpana.com

Vocational Rehabilitation Counselor

A vocational rehabilitation counselor assists a disabled person toward the full utilization of his or her employment potential through counseling and rehabilitation therapies. Vocational rehabilitation counselors practice in rehabilitation centers; federal, state, and local government agencies; mental hospitals; and educational institutions.

- **Educational Requirements.** A master's degree in rehabilitation counseling is required for this position.
- **The Need.** The outlook for this position is fair, as budget cutbacks have decreased the job hiring for rehabilitation counselors.
- **Number in the Field.** 24,000

• **Salaries.** Salaries range from $24,000 to $32,000. An experienced vocational rehabilitation counselor may earn as much as $60,000 annually.

For further information write:

American Rehabilitation Counseling Association
American Personnel and Guidance Association
5999 Stevenson Avenue
Alexandria, VA 22304
nchrtm.okstate.edu/arca

6

SPECIALISTS IN RELATED SCIENCES AND TECHNOLOGIES

THE PRACTICE OF medicine involves extensive use of sophisticated devices and tests to diagnose the patient's illness. Technicians play a major role in the means of determining the body's functions, identifying the patient's illness, and generally assisting a physician in making a diagnosis. With the forward march of medicine, more and more sophisticated technology becomes available for medical diagnosis and treatment. With this new technology is created the need for more highly skilled technicians to operate the equipment and monitor the patient's condition. Literally every day there are new forms of tests available to physicians, but physicians do not conduct these tests themselves. They rely on trained personnel— the technicians. These members of the medical team report back to the physicians the test results.

There is a broad array of technician specialties including clinical laboratory personnel, radiologic technicians, and electrocardiographers who are all involved in diagnostic testing. There are also technicians who are primarily involved in therapy, including radiation therapy and respiratory therapy. There is a wide range of technicians in medicine. They require different knowledge and skills, but the need to be precise and accurate is critical in the technician's job performance.

Biomedical Engineer

The biomedical engineer is a professional who is responsible for the overall operation of the biomedical department, including the supervision of biomedical equipment technicians. This department supervises and maintains such equipment as EKG machines and IV infusion devices. The biomedical engineer's responsibilities include the safe management of medical devices, primarily those of the electronic type. He or she consults with physicians, nurses, and patients relative to the use of medical instrumentation, and advises the medical personnel about the purchase of equipment.

Biomedical engineers work in hospitals, research foundations, and medical, academic, industrial, and government laboratories.

- **Educational Requirements.** The B.S. degree in engineering is usually required, although some biomedical engineers are physicists or physiologists who have taken advanced training. An ability to communicate on many levels is essential for a person considering biomedical engineering as a profession.
- **The Need.** The biomedical field is developing rapidly and the opportunities are increasing.
- **Number in the Field.** 3,000
- **Salaries.** The starting salaries for an engineer with a bachelor's degree is $35,000, with a master's degree $40,000, and with a Ph.D. $50,000 per year.

For further information write:

Association for Advancement of Medical Instrumentation
1110 North Glebe Road, Suite 220
Arlington, VA 22201
aami.org

Biomedical Equipment Technician

The biomedical equipment technician installs, operates, repairs, maintains, and calibrates electronic biomedical equipment, which is used in the diagnosis and treatment of disease. He or she is also responsible for instructing medical personnel in the proper operation of the instruments. This technician must maintain a large inventory of instruments.

• **Educational Requirements.** Usually an associate's degree from a community or junior college is required. At present, licensing or certification is not required.
• **The Need.** There is an increasing need for biomedical equipment technicians as the complexity of hospital equipment continues to increase.
• **Number in the Field.** 19,000
• **Salaries.** The salary for a biomedical equipment technician ranges from $30,000 to $35,000.

For further information write:

Association for the Advancement of Medical Instrumentation
1110 North Glebe Road, Suite 220
Arlington, VA 22201
aami.org

Clinical Perfusionist

The clinical perfusionist is a skilled person who operates circulation equipment during a medical situation where it is necessary to temporarily replace the patient's circulatory or respiratory functions, i.e., as in heart surgery. This equipment regulates the patient's supply of oxygen, carbon dioxide, blood chemistry, and circulation throughout surgery. Also, the perfusionist may be required to operate the heart-lung machine, to administer anesthetics and other drugs, and to control body temperature of the patient. Perfusionists always work in a hospital setting. They are employed by hospitals, surgeons, or professional health organizations.

- **Educational Requirements.** Clinical perfusionists are trained in programs offered by hospitals, medical schools, and universities throughout the country. All of these programs require a high school diploma, with a strong background in the sciences, particularly biology and chemistry. Most programs give preference to students with some college science work or previous experience in respiratory therapy or medical terminology. Perfusionists must have skilled hands, a long concentration span, work well under stress, and be able to think and react quickly in emergencies.
- **The Need.** The need for perfusionists is increasing due to the emphasis on operations involving the heart and lungs.
- **Number in the Field.** 2,200
- **Salaries.** The salary range for a perfusionist is $37,000 to $50,000 a year.

For further information write:

American Board of Cardiovascular Perfusion
207 North Twenty-Fifth Avenue
Hattiesburg, MS 39401
abcp.org

Dental Laboratory Technician

A dental laboratory technician is responsible for constructing and repairing partial or complete dentures, bridges, crowns, and inlays, and performing dental restorations according to instructions from the dentist. Appliances that are used in straightening teeth are also constructed and repaired. Dental laboratory technicians may be generalists or many specialize in one or more phases of the work. Persons who wish to pursue a career as a dental laboratory technician should have good form and spatial perception, a well-developed sense of color perception, manual dexterity, and an ability to work with respect for detail and accuracy.

Dental laboratory technicians work in dental offices, commercial dental laboratories, military and industrial settings, and companies that manufacture dental prosthetic material. For those who prefer academia, there are opportunities in research and teaching.

• **Educational Requirements.** Training can be done as a generalist or specialist. On-the-job training for four years or a two-year associate's degree program from an accredited school is necessary to become certified. Certification involves successful completion of the National Board of Certification in Dental Technology.
• **The Need.** As the dental field expands, employment opportunities in this field are expected to be very good.

- **Number in the Field.** 22,000
- **Salaries.** The average range for an experienced technician is $25,000 to $35,000 per year.

For further information write:

National Association of Dental Laboratories
1530 Metropolitan Boulevard
Tallahassee, FL 32308
nadl.org

Diagnostic Medical Sonographer

Ultrasound is a procedure that aids a physician in diagnosing disease and injury. The procedure works through the use of sonic energy enabling the physician to visualize interior parts of the anatomy. It is the sonographer's job to position the patient and work the ultrasound machine to obtain the optimum diagnostic results. Using a patient's history and clinical data, the sonographer positions the patient and surveys the area to be studied with regard to sonographic information and anatomical and pathological relationships. Using this information he or she sets the machine that will produce the best visual picture of the area, makes a scan, and records the results on a permanent record. This is then used for anatomical and pathological interpretation by a physician. Patience, an interest in science, and the ability to act independently are important in this career. Diagnostic medical sonographers work in hospitals and research facilities.

- **Educational Requirements.** Educational training for this position depends upon a person's previous training and background. There is a one-year program, which includes course work in anatomy, pathology, and computer applications in ultrasound. The two year program has additional course work in medical records, health terminology, anatomy, physiology, patient care, and ethics. Upon graduation from the program, candidates take a written, practical, and oral examination given by the American Registry of Diagnostic Medical Sonographers. After successful completion of the exam, the person is then recognized as a registered diagnostic medical sonographer (R.D.M.S.).

- **The Need.** There is a great shortage of sonographers.
- **Number in the Field.** 5,200 (registered)
- **Salaries.** The annual starting salary for a staff sonographer is $30,000 to $42,000.

For further information write:

American Registry of Diagnostic Medical Sonographers
2368 Victory Parkway, Suite 510
Cincinnati, OH 45806
ardms.org

Dialysis Technician

Dialysis technicians help to care for patients who have kidney conditions that require hemodialysis. Hemodialysis is a procedure used to cleanse waste materials from the blood of a patient whose kidneys fail to remove this waste. Dialysis technicians maintain and repair dialysis equipment, monitor dialysis equipment and vital signs of patients, and record patient data.

- **Educational Requirements.** No formal training is required; however, high school students are encouraged to take courses in biology, chemistry, science, math, communications, and health-related courses. Preparation is done in programs in renal units of hospitals or dialysis centers. Dialysis technicians are not required to be registered, licensed, or certified.

- **The Need.** Need will increase through 2010.
- **Salaries.** The average salary is $32,000.

For further information write:

Board of Nephrology Examiners
P.O. Box 15945-282
Lenexa, KS 66285
goamp.com/bonent

Electrocardiograph (EKG) Technician

An electrocardiograph (EKG) technician works in a hospital's EKG laboratory or at a patient's bedside, recording with an electrocardiograph machine the action of the heart's muscles. The recordings assist a physician in diagnosing heart irregularities. An EKG technician sets up the machine and then attaches electrodes to specific areas of the body. After completing the recording, they send the completed recording to a cardiologist or physician for analysis and interpretation. An EKG technician should enjoy working with patients, have a sympathetic personality, and be able to work harmoniously with physicians and hospital staff.

EKG technicians work in hospitals, clinics, and physicians' offices.

- **Educational Requirements.** Depending on the desired skill level, EKG technicians may be trained in on-the-job training pro-

grams in hospitals, or in one- or two-year degree programs. T
are not required to have a license.

• **The Need.** The current job market for EKG technicians is
competitive.

• **Number in the Field.** 32,000

• **Salaries.** In major metropolitan areas in the northeastern part
of the country, the salaries for an EKG technician in a 250-bed hospital range from $25,000 to $35,000 per year with an average salary
of $25,000. Salaries are lower in the southern and western portions
of the country.

For further information write:

American Cardiology Association
9111 Old Georgetown Road
Bethesda, MD 20814
acc.org

Electroencephalographic (EEG)
Technologist/Technician

Electroencephalography (EEG) is the study and recording of the
electrical activity of the brain. It is used to diagnose diseases of the
brain. The technologist records the EEG activity of the patient by
attaching electrodes to the patient's scalp. The electrodes are then
attached to a recording instrument; the controls are set to provide
the optimum recording, and the machine then provides a written
record of the electrical activity of the patient's brain. During the
recording period, the patient is carefully observed and a record is
kept of his or her behavior. An understanding of the equipment in
use and knowledge of the diseases of the brain, along with manual

dexterity, are required of the technologist. After training has been completed, considerable initiative is expected from the technologist.

EEG technologists work in hospital EEG laboratories, in clinics, and in physicians' offices.

• **Educational Requirements.** At present, most training for an EEG technologist is done on-the-job. In the future, training is expected to cover a one-year period with six months devoted to instruction and six months of supervised practice. Formal training programs are from one to two years in length and may lead to an associate's degree. Certification by the American Board of EEG Technologists is not required but is highly desirable for advancement in the field.

• **The Need.** Electroencephalography is one of the top growing fields.

• **Number in the Field.** 15,000

• **Salaries.** Salaries depend upon the technologist's training, experience, and willingness to assume responsibility. Salaries for a registered technologist range from $32,000 to $48,000.

For further information write:

American Board of Certified and Registered Encephalographic
    Technicians and Technologists
Harris Hospital, EEG Department
1300 West Cannon
Ft. Worth, TX 76104

American Board of Registration of Electroencephalographic
    Technologists
c/o The Psychological Corporation
7500 Old Oak Boulevard
Cleveland, OH 44130

American Society of Electro-Neurodiagnostic Technologies
Sixth at Quint
Carroll, IA 51401

Clinical Electroencephalographic Technicians and Technologists
  Society
Valley Neurology Associates
4244 North Nineteenth Avenue
Phoenix, AZ 85015

Emergency Medical Technician (E.M.T.)/Paramedic

Emergency medical technicians work under the direction of a physician through a radio communication network in recognizing, assessing, and managing medical emergencies that occur away from hospitals or other medical settings. E.M.T.s are trained to recognize the condition of a patient and initiate the appropriate treatment for a variety of surgical and medical emergencies. While transporting the patient to the medical facility, the E.M.T. radios the patient's condition to the physician, records details relating to the care given, and gives a description of the incident that led to the injury. Individuals who desire to become emergency medical technicians should be able to work effectively under stressful situations and have good communication skills, physical stamina, and an interest in assisting people.

Emergency medical technicians work for ambulance services, fire departments, police departments, hospital emergency departments, private industry, and voluntary care services.

• **Educational Requirements.** Training for E.M.T. careers can be done on a full- or part-time basis. Training is initially done for

E.M.T.-ambulance, along with certification requirements. After achieving these, a person may apply for an E.M.T.-paramedic program. These programs involve six hundred to one thousand hours of didactic and clinical training. Some programs combine training for E.M.T.-ambulance and E.M.T.-paramedic. In these cases, the teaching and supervised practice portions must be completed before the field internship begins. All states require graduates of E.M.T.-paramedic programs to be certified. At present the National Registry of Emergency Medical Technicians recognizes three levels of E.M.T. competency.

• **The Need.** The growing expectation of prehospital care of victims of sudden illness or injury has increased the demand for E.M.T.s.

• **Number in the Field.** There are close to half a million trained individuals and more than 45,200 E.M.T.-paramedics.

• **Salaries.** The average annual salary is $30,000 to $40,000. Entry-level E.MT.s receive $20,000 to $25,000 a year.

Further information is best obtained through your local, county, or state health department.

National Registry of Emergency Medical Technicians
P.O. Box 29233
Columbus, OH 43229
nremt.org

Medical Laboratory Technologist/Technician

A medical laboratory technologist/technician is responsible for clinical tests that are done under the supervision of a physician or medical technologist, which include the areas of hematology, serology, blood banking, urinalysis, microbiology, and clinical chemistry. A person who is interested in this position should have a strong interest in the sciences, be able to work with precision and accuracy, have good vision to perform the visual testing necessary, and have a sense of responsibility and dependability.

Medical laboratory technicians work in the laboratories of hospitals, commercial laboratories, medical clinics, and physicians' offices. Medical laboratory technicians can specialize in various fields such as histology and cytology.

• **Educational Requirements.** An associate's college degree in the medical laboratory field or graduation from an accredited medical laboratory technology/technician program, which includes specified hours in clinical experience, is required.

• **The Need.** At the present there are more openings in these positions than there are graduates. There are more openings in rural areas than in cities.

• **Number in the Field.** 205,000 technicians and 45,450 (certified) technologists

• **Salaries.** The entry-level salary for a medical laboratory technician with an associate's degree is $27,000. Average earnings for those with experience are $28,000 to $32,000. The entry-level salary for technologists is $33,000. Those with experience can earn $35,000 to $50,000.

For further information write:

American Medical Technologists
710 Higgins Road
Park Ridge, IL 60068
amt1.com

Medical Physicist

Medical physics is a subfield of physics that deals with the application of the field's concepts, methods, and forces for use in the diagnosis and treatment of disease. A medical physicist works in the area of research, teaching, and consultation with physicians. Working with other specialists, the physicist develops medical instruments by applying the principles of biology and physics and work assessment and control of radiation hazards. Persons who aspire to become medical physicists should possess intellectual curiosity, sound judgment, the ability to apply the scientific method in solving problems, and developed powers of observation and analysis.

Medical physicists work in universities, colleges, medical centers, hospitals, and in industry.

- **Educational Requirements.** A bachelor's degree, with courses in the physical and biological sciences, is the usual entrance requirement. Advanced degrees are offered in programs of medical physics or radiological physics. Practical experience is obtained through a traineeship program lasting one to two years.
- **The Need.** Growth in this field remains strong.
- **Number in the Field.** 46,500
- **Salaries.** The average starting salary is $50,000 a year. The average primary salary for a medical physicist is $89,000.

For further information write:

American Association of Physicists in Medicine
One Physics Ellipse
College Park, MD 20740
aapm.org

Microbiologist

Microbiologists cultivate, identify, and classify the microorganisms that are found in fluids, skin, and surgical specimens in a patient's body. These data are then used to identify or look for a cause, cure, or the prevention of a disease. Microbiologists also train and supervise microbiology technologists and technicians to work in the hospital laboratory. After all tests have been done on a patient's specimens, they post the findings and write a diagnostic report for the pathologist. Microbiologists also may work in finding the distribution patterns and method of transportation of bacteria. Microbiology has many different subspecializations: medical, clinical, veterinary, public health, immunology, virology, microbial physiology, biochemistry, molecular microbiology, and mycology. Supervisory skills, good vision and form perception, patience, and accuracy are necessary for this position.

Microbiologists work in a variety of settings: hospitals, clinics, private medical laboratories, government agencies, and in industry.

- **Educational Requirements.** Preparation for a career in microbiology is varied depending upon the type of position and responsibility. A bachelor's degree in science is the usual entry requirement and allows an individual to assist in research and perform routine analyses. Also, a B.S. in medical technology may be required for persons interested in working in a hospital or clinical setting. Some employers may require certification by the American Board of Microbiology of the American Academy of Microbiology. For positions involving independent research or teaching, a master's degree or Ph.D. is necessary.

- **The Need.** Doctoral degree holders can expect to face competition for basic research positions between 2002 and 2012.

Recent budget increases at the National Institutes of Health have led to large increases in federal basic research and development expenditures, with research grants growing both in number and in dollar amount. Currently, about one in three grant proposals are approved for long-term research projects. Opportunities for those with a bachelor's or master's degree in biological science are expected to be better. The number of science-related jobs in sales, marketing, and research management, for which non-Ph.D.s usually qualify, is expected to exceed the number of independent research positions. Biological scientists enjoyed very rapid gains in employment between the mid-1980s and mid-1990s, in part reflecting increased staffing requirements in new biotechnology companies.

- **Number in the Field.** 66,000 (biological scientists)
- **Salaries.** Microbiologists with a bachelor's degree start at about $25,000 to $36,000 a year; a master's degree receives a salary ranging from $35,000 to $58,000; and a microbiologist with a doctorate can earn up to $75,000 a year.

For further information write:

American Society for Microbiology
1752 N Street NW
Washington, DC 20036
asm.org

Nuclear Medicine Technologist/Technician

Nuclear medicine technology is concerned with the use of radioactive isotopes for diagnostic, therapeutic, and research purposes. The procedures in this field are used to perform body function studies and organ imaging, treat diseases, and analyze biologic specimens. The responsibilities of the technologist vary with typical tasks including quality control, preparing and administering radiopharmaceuticals, operating radiation detection instruments, correctly positioning the patient, proper imaging procedures, collecting and preparing biologic specimens, and preparing the information for use by a physician. A nuclear medicine technologist may be either a staff technologist or chief technologist, depending upon education and experience. Verbal and numerical skills, spatial perception, manual dexterity, and the ability to work with accuracy are important in this career.

Nuclear medicine technologists work in hospitals, public health institutions, research institutions, doctors' offices, and in teaching positions in colleges and universities.

• **Educational Requirements.** There are two programs that prepare a person for a career as a nuclear medicine technologist/technician. A two-year associate's degree is used for preparation as a technician, and a four-year program or bachelor's degree program prepares technologists. Graduation from an American Medical Association–approved program in nuclear medicine technology with a registry examination permits practice in the field. A person may also prepare for the field in other manners: graduation from a medical technology program with one year of experience in a clinical radioscope laboratory; a bachelor of science degree in biology, physical science, or chemistry with two years of experience; two years of college with specified science courses with four years of experience; or a high school diploma with six years of experience. All the routes also require a registry examination.

• **The Need.** The field of nuclear medicine technology is growing rapidly, and there is a demand for competent technologists. Current projections indicate 1,300 openings per year, 300 more than are currently graduating.

- **Number in the Field.** 25,000
- **Salaries.** Salaries will vary considerably depending on the type of institution, education, and geographic location. Starting salaries average about $27,000 a year. A certified or registered technologist with experience can earn between $32,000 and $42,000 a year.

For further information write:

Society of Nuclear Medicine
1850 Samuel Morse Drive
Reston, VA 20190
snm.org

Optician

Opticians (also called ophthalmic dispensers) receive lens prescriptions from ophthalmologists or optometrists, determine the type of eyeglasses that are desired by the patient, and order the lenses from ophthalmic laboratory technicians. Upon receiving the finished lenses, they use special equipment to check their power and surface quality. They then adjust the glass frames to the patient's face and head. In some states they may also fit contact lenses. As this type of work involves constant contact with patients, a pleasant personality and good interpersonal skills are required.

Opticians work in retail optical stores or department stores that sell prescription lenses. Others work for ophthalmologists or optometrists, in hospital eye clinics, or teach in schools of ophthalmic dispensing. Many opticians open their own retail optical shops after working in the field for a few years.

• **Educational Requirements.** Employers prefer an individual who has completed a two-year formal training course that leads to an associate's degree. High school graduates can enter the field through a two- to four-year formal apprenticeship program. Opticians may also learn their skills through on-the-job training. All states have individual licensing requirements to practice as an optician. The licensing exam involves meeting minimum standards of education and/or training and successful completion of a written practical exam.

• **The Need.** Opticianry is one of the most job-secure occupations. The number of opticianry jobs looks good through the year 2012.

• **Number in the Field.** 19,000

• **Salaries.** Annual salaries for opticians range from $30,000 to $35,000.

For further information write:

Opticians Association of America
7023 Little River Turnpike, Suite 207
Annandale, VA 22003
oaa.org

Optometric Technician

An optometric technician is trained to test vision, order lenses as prescribed by the doctor, determine the power of corrective lenses, take facial and frame measurements, and counsel patients on procedures and eye exercises. Maintaining patient records, billing, and bookkeeping are also part of the job. Optometric technicians have more extensive training than optometric assistants.

Optometric technicians and assistants work for doctors in private practice, in health clinics, in the armed forces, in health maintenance organizations, and in government agencies.

- **Educational Requirements.** Optometric technicians are required to have two years of study in a community college, technical school, or a college of optometry. They are required to be licensed or certified.
- **The Need.** At present there are more positions than there are trained people. Employment prospects are very good. More employment opportunities in the future will favor those who have graduated from formal training programs.
- **Number in the Field.** 57,000
- **Salaries.** The average salary for an optometric technician is $27,500.

For further information write:

American Optometric Association
243 North Lindbergh Boulevard
St. Louis, MO 63141
aoanet.org

Pharmacist

A pharmacist is a professional who has studied the science of drugs and dispenses medication and health supplies to the public. These individuals know the composition of drugs, both their chemical and physical properties, and understand what effects the medication will have on a person who is well or sick. He or she also is familiar with the companies that manufacture these drugs. Increasingly, pharmacists serve as sources of information to the public on effects of prescription and nonprescription medications. Intelligence, an interest in science, integrity, and strong communication skills are necessary.

Pharmacists are employed in a variety of settings: hospitals, clinics, nursing homes, government, pharmaceutical companies, sales research, teaching positions, and their own businesses.

- **Educational Requirements.** To receive a bachelor's degree in pharmacy requires five years of specialized study at a college or university. Advanced degrees also are granted. Such advanced degrees vary in length from one to five years, depending on the type of degree required. Master's of science and doctorate degrees may be obtained, which further enhance the opportunities of the pharmacist, especially in the area of the pharmaceutical industry.
- **The Need.** The supply and demand of pharmacists in the marketplace are just about even. Potential pharmacists will be placed with relative ease.
- **Number in the Field.** 172,000
- **Salaries.** The entry-level salary is about $39,500 per year. For experienced pharmacists the average salary is $52,000.

For further information write:

American Pharmaceutical Association
2215 Constitution Avenue
Washington, DC 20037
aphanet.org

Pharmacologist

Pharmacology is the science that deals with the properties and reactions drugs have on living systems. A pharmacologist performs tests to determine the therapeutic value of a drug, researches and develops new drugs, or improves on existing drugs. Research and development constitutes a major portion of a pharmacologist's work. An interest in science and the ability to do research-oriented work are necessary in this position.

Pharmacologists work in medical schools, universities, research institutes and foundations, pharmaceutical companies, and also hospitals.

- **Educational Requirements.** A bachelor's degree is the minimum entry requirement. Graduate degrees are necessary for research and teaching positions.
- **The Need.** There is a need for pharmacologists, especially those who specialize in immunology, molecular, and drug-abuse pharmacology.
- **Number in the Field.** 16,500
- **Salaries.** The starting salary for a pharmacologist with a bachelor's degree is between $35,000 and $45,000. The average salary for pharmacologists with experience is $48,000 a year.

For further information write:

American Society for Pharmacology and Experimental
    Therapeutics, Inc.
9650 Rockville Pike
Bethesda, MD 20814
aspet.org

Radiologic (X-Ray) Technician

The radiologic technician, or radiographer, assists the radiologist in the process of taking x-ray films. These films are used by the radiologist to examine the patient for broken bones, tumors, ulcers, malfunction of organs, and disease. The radiographer positions the patient to expose the correct portion of the body for filming, adjusts the x-ray equipment to the correct setting, and takes the desired number of pictures. He or she may also give a patient certain chemical mixtures so that body organs will appear on the x-ray film. The radiographer usually works directly in the radiology department of a hospital, but he or she may use mobile x-ray equipment in the patient's room or in surgery. The ability to communicate clearly in working with patients and responsibility to handle the x-ray film and equipment are necessary in this career.

Radiographers work in hospitals, laboratories, clinics, physicians' offices, government agencies, and in industry.

• **Educational Requirements.** Training for the career is done in a two- or four-year accredited hospital or college course. Some colleges are now offering a Bachelor of Science Degree in Radiologic Technology. After training has been completed, certification is done by the American Registry of Radiologic Technologists. Successful completion of the examination enables the person to become a registered radiographer. Radiographers may also elect to receive special on-the-job training in magnetic resonance imaging (MRI). An A.S. or A.A.S. degree in radiography or a two-year hospital-based program leading to certified radiography is required.

• **The Need.** Job opportunities for radiologic technicians are expected to be favorable. Radiologic technologists who also are experienced in more complex diagnostic imaging procedures, such as CT or MRI, will tend to have better employment opportunities. Employment of radiologic technologists and technicians is expected to grow faster than the average for all occupations through 2012 as the population grows and ages, thus increasing the demand for diagnostic imaging.

- **Number in the Field.** 215,000 radiologic (x-ray) technicians
- **Salaries.** A radiographer earns between $27,000 and $40,000.

For further information write:

American Society of Radiologic Technologists
3420 East Twelfth Street
Des Moines, IA 50216
isrt.org

7

MANAGEMENT AND
ADMINISTRATION WORKERS

HEALTH ADMINISTRATION IS really the central component of the management of health programs, services, institutions, and agencies. Many of the people engaged in management of health services are recognized as professionals under the umbrella of health services administration including its major component, hospital administration. Health administration is a broad term. It encompasses the management of varied activities including planning, organizing, controlling, and supervising, as well as evaluating institutional and community resources, systems, and procedures by which the needs and demands of the health and medical systems are met.

Management is the directing of various functions in the institutions, programs, and services that help to make the health organization work. Depending on the size of the institution, administrators do this personally in smaller operations and by working through a staff of assistants in larger institutions.

Health administrators are called upon to make many decisions; for example, they may approve budgets and negotiate contracts. Assistant hospital administrators may direct the daily operations of various departments, such as the food service, housekeeping, and maintenance departments.

More specifically, hospital administrators, whether they are employed at a large urban hospital or a small rural facility, are responsible for managing the entire hospital operations and all its related units. The chief administrator is hired by a board of trustees or other governing authority and is responsible for seeing that the board's policies are carried out. The chief administrator then hires other managers in the organization to carry out departmental administrative duties.

Administrative Roles

Administrators assume various roles while managing, but most administrators fit into all or one of three specific roles. These roles are business manager, institutional coordinator, or chief executive. To some degree, most administrators assume a part in all of these roles. In the business manager role, the administrator is responsible for many of the institution's internal operations. This means that he or she must order and procure supplies, manage personnel, and provide physicians and other health care professionals with the resources they need to do their jobs. In this role the administrator is also concerned with financial and statistical data—the basic reports of the hospital's financial affairs. This side of an administrator's work uses his or her ability to understand statistics and finance.

As a coordinator, the administrator has to develop more of an outside role. The administrator may become more influential as a negotiator, particularly with insurance plans that pay the patients' hospital bills. Being active in public relations is also part of this coordinator's role. In this capacity administrators work with very diverse groups. They may be seen with physicians chatting about a problem on the medical staff, or making administrative rounds and keeping in touch with employees or patients. Perhaps the most important tool of the administrator as coordinator is communications. Communicating in writing, orally in public speaking, or over the telephone are all important in getting the job done successfully.

Employees, staff, and the public have a right to expect the administrator to look the part of an executive. This means the administrator must be well groomed and dressed appropriately. The dress style could be conservative as it is in many agencies or institutions, or less formal, which is common in some parts of the country. The important element is that the administrator be dressed appropriately for the time and situation.

The executive as administrator has brought about some title changes to the position. The chief administrator may carry the title "executive director," "executive vice-president," or "president." As you can see from the number of titles, the definition of health administration is quite broad. It encompasses the management of many and varied institutions and tasks. But all institutions have one thing in common; they provide medical and health services.

Health Administration as a Profession

In 1939 the American Hospital Association and the American College of Hospital Administrators jointly produced a code of ethics for hospitals and administrators. This gave hospital and health administration one of the principles needed to grow as a profession. Since this time, there have been numerous indications of its growth, including the publication of a variety of well-respected technical and professional journals in the field. This adds to the specialized body of knowledge for management and planning of health services. Also, there is highly specialized professional education available to those seeking to enter the field of health administration. There are also a number of professional societies that are well established in the field: the American College of Hospital Administrators, the American College of Nursing Home Administrators, and the American College of Clinic Management, as well as the Association of Mental Health Administrators and a Health Administration section of the American Public Health Association. These are just a few of the professional administrative associations.

Management and Administration in Hospitals

The opportunities for administration in a hospital are not limited to the few executive jobs at the top; many other challenging and diversified management jobs exist in today's hospital. Because of rapid continuing growth in the health care field and the trend toward specialization, many new administrative positions must be filled to effectively operate today's hospital. Scientific and medical gains have had an impact on all health professions and occupations, including those in management. Some management positions require a degree of technical knowledge, but many can be learned with a combination of formal schooling and on-the-job experience. One example is the executive housekeeper. Other administrative jobs offer specialists practical experience in their primary occupations as well as the opportunity to manage people and other resources. Nurses, pharmacists, accountants, and many other professionals are all candidates for this type of administrative position.

Certain key hospital administrative positions in the executive, finance, support, nursing, and planning and marketing departments are reviewed here.

Chief Executive Officer (CEO)/Administrator

The chief executive officer is responsible for the overall functioning of the organization and for adherence to the organization's mission. This person develops and implements strategic plans for maintaining and/or improving delivery of services.

- **Educational Requirements.** A master's degree in business administration or related field is often a minimal requirement. Training and experience in medicine, nursing, or a related business/finance field is often helpful.
- **The Need.** Hospitals are in a consolidation and downsizing period. The need for hospital CEOs is declining. The need for hospital systems CEOs will become greater.
- **Number in the Field.** 6,250
- **Salaries.** $170,000 to $210,000

For further information write:

American College of Healthcare Executives
One North Franklin, Suite 1700
Chicago, IL 60606
ache.org

Chief Operations Officer (COO)/Administrative Officer

The chief operations officer is responsible for the day-to-day operations carried out by the organization. This person acts in place of the CEO/administrator when he or she is not available.

- **Educational Requirements.** A master's degree in business administration or a related field is often a minimal requirement. Training and experience in medicine, nursing, or a related business/finance field is often helpful.
- **The Need.** Because hospitals are downsizing the COO positions are on the decline.
- **Number in the Field.** 4,570
- **Salaries.** $120,000 to $150,000

For further information write:

American College of Healthcare Executives
One North Franklin
Chicago, IL 60606
ache.org

Chief Financial Officer (CFO)

The chief financial officer is responsible for developing and implementing the organization's financial plan and for implementing accounting and budgeting policies. This person directs processes whereby departments develop budgets, track expenses, record and collect revenues, and maintain financial statements.

- **Educational Requirements.** A baccalaureate or master's degree in accounting or finance is usually required. Experience in health care organizations is helpful. Often a C.P.A. is required.
- **The Need.** The need for CFOs is declining at about the same rate as other hospital executives. There is an increasing need for hospital systems CFOs.
- **Number in the Field.** 6,500
- **Salaries.** $100,000 to $180,000

For further information write:

Healthcare Financial Management Association
Two Westbrook Corporate Center, Suite 700
Westchester, IL 60154
hfma.org

Chief Nursing Officer (CNO)

The chief nursing officer directs nursing staff planning, recruitment, and development. This person coordinates activities of nursing staff with those of other areas, implements the organization's policies with respect to delivery of nursing services, and oversees the nursing budget.

- **Educational Requirements.** A baccalaureate or master's in nursing is required. Experience in hospital nursing and staffing is a requisite.
- **The Need.** Because of consolidation in hospital management, CNOs are declining as are other hospital positions. There is an increased demand for CNOs in outpatient activities.
- **Number in the Field.** 6,600
- **Salaries.** $95,000 to $120,000

For further information write:

American Organization of Nurse Executives (AONE)
One North Franklin, 34th Floor
Chicago, IL 60606
aone.org

Chief Medical Officer (CMO)/Medical Director

The chief medical officer directs medical staff planning, recruitment, and development. This person acts as liaison between administration and medical staffs, and implements the organization's policies with respect to delivery of medical services.

- **Educational Requirements.** An M.D. or D.O. is required. Often the position is filled by physicians who have practiced medicine. Understanding and strong communication skills are usually required. It is helpful if the physician has had experience in teaching residents and interns.
- **The Need.** The need for physician executives—CMOs—has remained steady. An increasing number of physicians are moving full-time or part-time into medical management.
- **Number in the Field.** 1,750 to 2,500
- **Salaries.** $130,000 to $170,000

Long-Term Care/Nursing Home Administrator

A long-term care nursing home administrator is the person responsible for the overall operation of a nursing home or other long-term care facility. This position involves making decisions that affect the welfare of the nursing home residents and staff. As the top manager in the institution, the administrator sets the pace, attitude, and quality of care of the institution. Working under the policies established by the board of trustees or the owner, the nursing home administrator directs the activities of the various departments; prepares monthly financial reports; establishes the budget; hires, supervises, and establishes training programs for new employees; and ensures that the home is in compliance with governmental regulations. Outside the nursing home, he or she must engage in public relations contact with the community. An ability to work with all types of individuals and organizational, supervisory, communication, and numerical skills are necessary for this position.

Nursing home administrators work in nursing homes and in the corporate offices of nursing home chains.

• **Educational Requirements.** A college degree, while not necessary, is the usual education desired. Ideally the administrator will have course work in long-term care, gerontology, or nursing home administration. Usually an internship under a licensed nursing home administrator is required. In all cases the administrator must be licensed by the respective State Board of Examiners for Nursing Home Administrators.

• **The Need.** As the number of elderly increases in the country, there will be an increasing need for nursing homes and nursing home administrators.

• **Number in the Field.** 29,000

• **Salaries.** Salaries for a nursing home administrator range between $38,000 and $75,000.

For further information write:

American College of Health Care Administrators
300 North Lee Street, Suite 301
Alexandria, VA 22314
achca.org

Hospital Controller

A controller is the head of the fiscal division of the hospital. The controller is responsible for the entire area of the institution's financial management, which includes budgeting, bookkeeping, general accounting activities, crediting, and collecting on patients' bills. The controller may work closely with both the hospital administrator and the board of trustees, informing these parties of the institution's financial status and its future trends in this area.

• **Educational Requirements.** A bachelor's degree in accounting or business administration is the minimum educational requirement. Some supervisory responsibility would be helpful. Certain hospitals might require a C.P.A.

• **The Need.** Because of hospital consolidation, the need for hospital controllers is declining. Because of hospital downsizing, the field will see more combined positions of CFO and controller.

• **Number in the Field.** 2,550 to 3,500

• **Salaries.** $72,000 to $80,000

For further information write:

Healthcare Financial Management Association
Two Westbrook Corporate Center, Suite 700
Westchester, IL 60154
hfma.org

Director, Patient Accounts

This person supervises the patients' accounts branch of the hospital's financial area.

• **Educational Requirements.** A college degree or some college courses in either business administration or accounting are considered desirable. Several years' experience in credit and collection work is preferred by most hospitals.

- **The Need.** Positions are holding steady or increasing, but there is a major shift from inpatient to outpatient accounts.
- **Number in the Field.** 5,200 to 6,100
- **Salaries.** $62,000 to $70,000

For further information write:

American Guild of Patient Account Management
1101 Connecticut Avenue NW, Suite 700
Washington, DC 20036
healthcarejobs.org

Director of Admissions

The admitting officer is in charge of the admitting department and is responsible for supervising and coordinating all the departmental operations. One of the manager's main functions is to select, train, and supervise the admitting personnel.

- **Educational Requirements.** A college degree in business administration or social science would be helpful. One or two years of prior work in an admitting department are required. Some hospitals may employ a nurse as the admitting officer.
- **The Need.** The need is declining due to hospital consolidation and the decrease in hospital admission and outpatient assistance.
- **Number in the Field.** 4,550
- **Salaries.** $52,000 to $62,000

For further information write:

American Hospital Association
One North Franklin
Chicago, IL 60606
aha.org

Director of Managed Care

The director directs and coordinates the development of managed care strategies and activities for a medical center and its affiliates. This person advises and consults with operating departments to handle managed care requirements. The director also coordinates with practice groups and clinical departments managed care opportunities for specific services and programs such as occupational health and substance abuse services.

• **Educational Requirements.** Generally a baccalaureate degree is required though not mandatory. Individuals with nursing and insurance backgrounds are often considered. An understanding of contracting, financing, and quality assurance is helpful.

• **The Need.** One of the fastest-growing positions in the hospital is managed care. This increase is directly proportional to the shift of patients into managed care organizations.

• **Number in the Field.** 1,500 to 2,000

• **Salaries.** $60,000 to $80,000

For further information write:

American College of Healthcare Executives
One North Franklin, Suite 1700
Chicago, IL 60606
ache.org

Director of Human Resources

This person manages the hospital's personnel department functions. This department head is responsible for the recruitment, selection, and placement of employees within the institution. The personnel director has the responsibilities of developing personnel policies and procedures on working conditions, employment practices, pay scales, and grievance procedures. The personnel department is also responsible for providing employee orientation programs and establishing training programs.

- **Educational Requirements.** A bachelor's degree is generally required with a major in business administration, personnel administration, or industrial relations. Work toward a master's degree will enable a person to advance more rapidly. Courses in tests and measurements as well as applied psychology are helpful. The ability to analyze job situations and to effectively communicate with people is important in this position.
- **The Need.** The number for this position is declining, as with other hospital administration positions.
- **Number in the Field.** 4,550 to 5,500
- **Salaries.** $82,000 to $89,000

For further information write:

American Society for Healthcare Human Resources Administration
c/o American Hospital Association
One North Franklin
Chicago, IL 60606
hospitalconnect.com

Purchasing Director/Materials Manager

The purchasing director or chief resource officer is responsible for supervising and directing a program to purchase the necessary supplies, materials, and equipment to keep the hospital functioning properly. This involves supervising the storage, control, and issuance of supplies to the various hospital departments. The director must also maintain contacts with the hospital's vendors and keep up to date on prices, trends, and the availability of supplies and new products.

- **Educational Requirements.** Usually the position calls for a manager who has graduated from college with a degree in business administration or a related field. Courses in accounting, marketing, and purchasing are helpful. Knowledge of applied business economics and business practices is also desirable.
- **The Need.** The number for this position is declining due to hospital consolidation and downsizing.
- **Number in the Field.** 5,000 to 6,000
- **Salaries.** $75,000 to $110,000

For further information write:

Association for Healthcare Resource and Materials Management
One North Franklin
Chicago, IL 60606
hospitalconnect.com

Food Service Administrator

The food service administrator may also be called the "administrative dietitian." It is this department head's job to direct and coordinate the food preparation for the hospital. The manager is also responsible for the preparation of special diets for patients. Responsibilities include supervising personnel, requisitioning food and supplies, and maintaining records.

- **Educational Requirements.** The food service administrator should have a college degree in nutrition, business administration, or a related field. Being familiar with large-scale food operations like those found in universities and hospitals is also necessary. An understanding of quality controls in the purchasing and preparation of food is desirable.
- **The Need.** The need is declining due to hospital consolidation and mergers. Many of these positions will be outsourced to large food service companies.
- **Number in the Field.** 5,200 to 5,900
- **Salaries.** $56,500 to $59,500

For further information write:

American Society for Healthcare Food Service Administrators
One North Franklin
Chicago, IL 60606
hospitalconnect.com

Executive Housekeeper

The supervision and direction of the institution's housekeeping program is the responsibility of the executive housekeeper. The person in this management position must set the standards of cleanliness throughout the hospital. Establishing work methods and systems, preparing cleaning schedules, and hiring and training the housekeeping department employees are part of this administrator's job.

The hospital's laundry service may also be part of this person's responsibility.

- **Educational Requirements.** To be certified for membership in the National Executive Housekeepers' Association, it is necessary to hold a high school diploma. College courses in management are also helpful. Knowledge of the hospital's operations and a thorough understanding of building materials and equipment are important in this position. Supervision of employees is a key part of this manager's role.
- **The Need.** The need is declining due to hospital consolidation and mergers. Many of these positions will be outsourced to large housekeeping companies.
- **Number in the Field.** 5,000 to 6,000
- **Salaries.** $50,000 to $60,000

For further information write:

American Hospital Association
One North Franklin
Chicago, IL 60606
hospitalconnect.com

Director of Volunteer Services

The director of volunteer services directs and coordinates the efforts of the volunteers in the hospital. To do this, the department head must establish a volunteer program in conjunction with the various hospital departments that use volunteer services. The director of the volunteer department organizes formal instructional programs for volunteers to orient and teach them proper hospital procedures and techniques.

• **Educational Requirements.** Usually the director of this department has a college education. It could be helpful to have taken courses in management, sociology, and psychology. Training in public relations and public speaking would be very helping in this position. Most hospitals prefer that their director of volunteers have some supervisory experience, experience as a volunteer, and/or have participated in some community organization work.

• **The Need.** The need is declining and is directly proportional to the downsizing of hospitals.

• **Number in the Field.** 3,500+

• **Salaries.** $52,000 to $58,000

For further information write:

American Society of Directors of Volunteer Services
c/o American Hospital Association
One North Franklin
Chicago, IL 60606
hospitalconnect.com

Care/Case Manager

The case manager identifies inpatients at high risk of re-admission and works with patients during inpatient stay to achieve maximum independence upon discharge. The manager develops the multi-disciplinary care plan (critical paths) in collaboration with other members of the health care team and coordinates with social workers to arrange community support services for high-risk patients following discharge. He or she also provides support and counseling to the patient and his or her family.

- **Educational Requirements.** Generally a baccalaureate or master's in nursing is required. Experience in patient care and understanding of teaching and research skills could be helpful.
- **The Need.** This executive nurse position continues to grow as subordinate positions are consolidated. The need for this position is increasing rapidly in outpatient areas.
- **Number in the Field.** 20,000 to 25,000
- **Salaries.** $55,000 to $65,000

For further information write:

American Nurses Association
600 Maryland Avenue SW, Suite 100
Washington, DC 20024
nursingworld.org

Risk Manager

The hospital risk manager is a member of the administration who works closely with the nursing service and the nursing units. It is the manager's job to implement and coordinate the institution's risk management program. The manager uses insurance company reports, hospital incident reports, licensing and accrediting agencies' surveys and audits, as well as his or her own inspections to structure ways the hospital can lower its risk and improve its environment.

- **Educational Requirements.** A baccalaureate degree may be required, but strong experience in quality assurance and risk management and insurance is mandatory. This position has broad exposure to the hospital and requires strong communication skills.

- **The Need.** This position is on the decline directly proportional to hospital consolidation and downsizing.
- **Number in the Field.** 2,500 to 3,000
- **Salaries.** $65,000 to $75,000

For further information write:

American Society for Healthcare Risk Management
c/o American Hospital Association
One North Franklin
Chicago, IL 60606
hospitalconnect.com

Quality Assurance Director

The quality assurance director is in charge of the hospital's quality assurance program. This department head will maintain a system of control over the utilization of the facility, including monitoring patients' length of stay and the appropriateness of services patients receive. The department will publish criteria for medical audit and reviews. The director will work with the various hospital and medical staff committees to review and improve patient care. The manager will retain records and profiles on patient care and utilization studies performed.

For further information write:

Society for Healthcare Planning and Marketing
American Hospital Association
One North Franklin
Chicago, IL 60606
hospitalconnect.com

Director of Planning

The director of planning develops marketing plans for the organization, including plans for new services and adaptation of existing services to better serve the client population.

- **Educational Requirements.** Often a baccalaureate or master's degree is required. Familiarity with health care is helpful. This individual must have strong quantitative skills.
- **The Need.** The need for this position is decreasing. There is job consolidation with the director of marketing positions.
- **Number in the Field.** 2,500 to 3,000
- **Salaries.** $88,000 to $93,000

Director of Public Relations

This director implements the organization's public relations activities, including advertising and press releases.

- **Educational Requirements.** A baccalaureate degree or more is required, as is experience in marketing and public relations. Strong written and oral communications skills and the ability to be an effective liaison with the media are necessary.
- **The Need.** The need for this position is relatively steady. Its increased activity is in the outpatient area.
- **Number in the Field.** 5,000 to 6,000
- **Salaries.** $65,000 to $75,000

Director of Marketing

The marketing specialist is responsible for projects and tasks relating to market research, planning, and promotion; interpretation of patient/customer/physician attitudes, values, and expectations; assessment of current programs; and testing of the clinical, operational, financial, ethical, medical, and legal feasibility of proposed programs.

- **Educational Requirements.** A baccalaureate degree or higher is recommended, as well as experience in health care and planning. Marketing experience and public relations skills are essential.
- **The Need.** The need for this position is decreasing proportionate to hospital consolidation and downsizing.
- **Number in the Field.** Approximately 4,000
- **Salaries.** $62,000 to $98,250

Director of Development

It is the director of development's job to develop programs that will increase the amount of political, community, and financial support. Other duties include planning and implementing fund-raising efforts, such as specific projects and activities that are a part of annual or capital campaigns, as well as evaluating fund-raising programs. This position requires excellent communication skills and techniques and the ability to assess constituency, consumer attitudes, expectations, and level of support.

- **Educational Requirements.** A baccalaureate degree or extensive fund-raising experience and the ability to communicate effectively are essential.
- **The Need.** The need for this position is decreasing directly proportional to hospital consolidation and downsizing. The need for this position at the hospital systems level is increasing.
- **Number in the Field.** 3,500 to 4,500
- **Salaries.** $73,500 to $85,000

8

HOSPITAL AND HEALTH CARE
SERVICES AND OPERATIONS

THERE IS A wide range of opportunities in medical care concerned with sophisticated equipment, logistics, materials, and goods. The interests and skills required to work with this array are different than those used when dealing in administration or when dealing directly with patients.

Some of these occupations are closely related to scientific research. Others cross over between some of the basic tasks performed by therapist and technician. One of the high profile occupations in this category is involved in biomedical activities. Biomedical engineering is one of the specialties that came about as a result of advances in science and engineering within the medical and health fields. A variety of devices are used in medical care, and they all need to be repaired. There are great opportunities here. Many occupations are related to computer technology, a growing field in itself. There are many opportunities to be found in hospitals.

A review of the dollar commitment made by our medical care system in diagnostic and therapeutic equipment shows that the nation's hospitals will spend almost six billion dollars in this area next year. Much of the emphasis is on repair and preventive maintenance of the equipment. The specialists working on these areas are also involved in training and orientation of nursing, medical staff, and other technical personnel on the potential and use of this equipment. Following is a description of these specialties.

Central Service Technician

The central service technician, also called central supply technician, supervises supply room employees in cleaning, sterilizing, storing, and issuing of instruments, equipment, and supplies according to established procedures and techniques. Equipment first is collected from operating rooms, delivery rooms, emergency units, nursing stations, and patient rooms and then is reprocessed and stored for future use. The central service technician also is responsible for disposable equipment. He or she must be conscientious, reliable, able to accept responsibility, and able to work at repetitive tasks. Manual dexterity is another important qualification as the job requires making repairs on and adjusting equipment. Central service technicians are employed in hospitals.

• **Educational Requirements.** On-the-job training for a three- to six-month period is the usual training for the position. This training includes instruction in medical terminology, chemistry, principles of steam and autoclaving, principles of cross infection, and safety.

• **Salaries.** The average salary is $14.25 per hour.

For further information write:

American Society for Hospital Central Service Personnel
American Hospital Association
One North Franklin Avenue
Chicago, IL 60606
hospitalconnect.com

Dietary Manager

A dietary manager participates, through assigned tasks, in supervising food service under the guidance of a registered dietitian, ADA dietitian, or a dietetic technician. This individual may plan menus according to established guidelines, supervise food production or service, procure and receive supplies, monitor food service for conformance with quality standards, and perform other related duties as designated.

Dietary managers work in hospitals, health care and community agencies, and in schools.

• **Educational Requirements.** A high school diploma and the successful completion of a dietetic assistant program approved by the American Dietetic Association are required.
• **The Need.** With the growing interest in better food preparation, dietary managers are in demand.
• **Number in the Field.** 17,250
• **Salaries.** The average salary is $36,814 in the northeastern United States.

For further information write:

Dietary Managers Association
406 Surrey Woods Drive
St. Charles, IL 60174
dmaonline.org

Dietetic Technician

A dietetic technician is a technically skilled person who works under the guidance of a registered dietitian or an ADA dietitian. This individual has responsibilities in assigned areas in food service management, in teaching food and nutritional principles, and in dietary counseling.

Dietetic technicians work in hospitals, health care and community agencies, and in schools.

- **Educational Requirements.** Successful completion of an associate's degree program that meets the educational standards established by the American Dietetic Association is required.
- **The Need.** An increasing emphasis on health and nutrition care has created a growing demand for these nutrition specialists.
- **Number in the Field.** 3,750
- **Salaries.** At a large urban hospital the average salary is $14.85 per hour.

For further information write:

American Dietetic Association
120 South Riverside Plaza, Suite 2000
Chicago, IL 60606
eatright.org

Hospital Engineer

The hospital engineer plans, directs, and supervises the daily and long-range operations of the engineering department, including troubleshooting in the mechanical areas. He or she is responsible for in-house construction and energy conservation projects.

• **Educational Requirements.** In smaller hospitals, on-the-job training is used. In larger hospitals, a college degree or equivalency in electrical or mechanical engineering is required. An individual usually serves several years as an assistant engineer or works in the building trades before assuming the top engineering post.

• **The Need.** There is a large number of hospital engineers, as most hospitals employ hospital engineers. Opportunities will occur as engineers retire or move into other fields.

• **Number in the Field.** 30,000

• **Salaries.** The average salary is $57,300 per year.

For further information write:

American Society for Hospital Engineers
American Hospital Association
840 North Lake Shore Drive
Chicago, IL 60611

Hospital Food Service Worker (Dietary Aide)

The food service worker is responsible for the preparation and serving of food to patients and employees. This job involves storing and preparing the food, serving in the cafeteria, washing the dishes, and cleaning the kitchen. As the hospital must meet specified sanitation standards, these functions must be done in a thorough manner.

Food service workers work in hospitals, nursing homes, and other health institutions that prepare and serve meals.

- **Educational Requirements.** Food service workers are trained on the job.
- **The Need.** Openings in food service positions will occur as people retire or move on to other positions.
- **Salaries.** The average salary is $14.00 per hour.

For further information contact the personnel department of your neighborhood hospital.

Hospital Housekeeping Worker

The housekeeping positions in a hospital include custodians, aides, and linen handlers. These workers perform light- and heavy-duty cleaning, do minor maintenance work, take care of the hospital linen, and do any lifting and moving. For these positions, physical stamina is required along with a dedication to sanitation and tidiness.

- **Educational Requirements.** A high school diploma is preferred. In most cases, on-the-job training is offered, which allows the employee the chance to earn while he/she learns. The employee should be able to demonstrate skills and knowledge of proper use of chemicals and equipment and be able to pass a mechanical aptitude test so that equipment malfunctions can be detected.
- **Salaries.** The average salary is $13.75 per hour.

For further information contact the personnel department of your neighborhood hospital.

Hospital Laundry Worker

A laundry worker works in the hospital laundry or in commercial establishments that contract to do the hospital laundry work. The tasks include collection, washing, drying, sorting, and pressing. The position requires a high degree of physical labor and manual dexterity. Laundry workers are employed in hospitals, nursing homes, and commercial laundry establishments.

- **Educational Requirements.** Laundry workers are trained on the job.
- **Salaries.** The average salary is $14.25 per hour.

For further information contact the personnel office of your neighborhood hospital.

Hospital Maintenance Worker

The hospital maintenance worker is responsible for keeping the hospital's power plant, building, equipment, and grounds in good condition. He or she may also work on equipment according to a preventive maintenance program to keep equipment running smoothly. Skill with tools and good mechanical abilities are necessary for this position. Maintenance workers are employed in all health institutions that have a physical plant and grounds.

- **Educational Requirements.** Training for these positions is conducted through formal apprenticeship programs. Licensing may be required for the plumbing and stationary engineer positions.
- **The Need.** There are many persons employed in the hospital maintenance field; openings will occur as persons move into other fields or retire.

- **Salaries.** The average salary is $16.80 per hour.

For further information contact the personnel department of your local hospital.

Medical Illustrator

A medical illustrator draws illustrations of parts of the human body for medical texts and slide presentations. A combined interest in art in addition to knowledge of biological and physical sciences are necessary. Usually medical illustrators work in art studios located in offices or their own homes.

- **Educational Requirements.** A bachelor's degree in fine arts is useful; however, specialized training for a medical illustrator is absolutely essential. A two-year associate's degree program or a vocational educational program will provide the technical skills necessary but may not give the background necessary for advancement.
- **The Need.** Competition is keen, but there is a need for medical illustrators who are talented.
- **Number in the Field.** 2,200
- **Salaries.** Salaries for a medical illustrator are quite variable, ranging between $40,000 and $75,000.

For further information write:

Association of Medical Illustrators
5475 Mark Dabling Boulevard, Suite 108
Colorado Springs, CO 80918
ami.org

Medical Records Technician

Medical records technicians organize, analyze, and evaluate medical and health records. In addition they compile various administrative and health statistics; code symptoms, diseases, operations, and procedures; transcribe medical reports; input and retrieve computerized health data; and control the use and release of health information. This position involves typing medical reports, preparing statistical reports on patients treated, supervising the clerical personnel, and handling "problem" requests for medical records information. This position also involves the training and orientation of new employees.

Medical records technicians are employed in hospitals, nursing homes, HMOs, physicians' offices, and government agencies.

• **Educational Requirements.** A two-year academic program for medical records technicians or the American Medical Association Independent Study Program, which is available only to applicants who are currently employed in a medical records department and who have a minimum of 30 semester hours of academic credits, is required. Candidates must pass the AMRA Accreditation Examination.

• **The Need.** The need for medical records technicians has increased with the expanding use of health care information.

• **Number in the Field.** 68,000

• **Salaries.** Entry-level salaries range from $20,000 to $30,000. The average is $25,000 to $35,000.

For further information write:

American Health Information Management Association
233 North Michigan Avenue, Suite 2150
Chicago, IL 60611
ahima.org

Registered Record Administrator

The registered record administrator is responsible for planning, organizing, and controlling the functions of the department for the purposes of maintaining the medical records of all patients, past and present, as well as providing services to the hospital staff. This is accomplished in a manner that is consistent with the medical, administrative, and legal requirements of the health care delivery system. The duties of the position include maintaining information systems within the health care facility, as well as with other health care practitioners, third party payers, and patients, in a manner that protects the patients' rights of confidentiality and privacy. Registered record administrators are involved in various aspects of overall hospital quality assurance through problem identification, assessment, and review; compiling statistical reports; assisting physicians in criteria development for medical audit; and in-service education. The registered record administrator also participates as an ex officio member of various committees of the medical staff. In addition, there are opportunities to develop health information systems for quality patient care, facility reimbursement, medical research, health planning, and health care evaluation.

Registered record administrators work in hospitals, ambulatory and long-term facilities, insurance companies, government agencies, universities, and in private consulting practice and enterprise (the technologies, such as consultant, computer, and word-processing companies).

• **Educational Requirements.** A high school graduate can take a four-year degree program in a university or college in health records administration. This program must be accredited by the Committee on Allied Health Education and Accreditation of the American Medical Association in collaboration with the Committee on Education and Registration of the American Medical Record Association. Upon completing the program, the graduate is eligible to take the AMRA's national examination to become a registered record administrator (R.R.A.). A college graduate, after meeting established prerequisites, may take an accredited one-year postgraduate certificate program in medical records administration and then take the AMRA's exam. Personal requirements for this position include integrity, sensitivity, organizational and motivational skills, and the ability to communicate with a variety of people.

• **The Need.** Advances in medical science, widespread computerization, and the need to manage health care facilities have created numerous employment opportunities for R.R.A.s.

• **Number in the Field.** 18,000

• **Salaries.** The salaries for a registered record administrator range from $20,000 to $75,000.

For further information write:

American Health Information Management Association
233 North Michigan Avenue, Suite 2150
Chicago, IL 60611
ahima.org

9

GETTING STARTED IN THE HEALTH AND MEDICAL PROFESSIONS

CHANCES ARE YOUR résumé will introduce you to your prospective employer. Because this first impression is so important, let us spend some time showing you how to present yourself attractively on paper. It is up to you to tell the prospective employer why he or she should hire you based on the following information: who you are, what you know, what you have done, and what you would like to do for the new employer. When creating your résumé, keep in mind that you must be able to support its contents. You may be requested to amplify your statements during a personal interview. Should this occur, you would be expected to add details without hesitation. Failure to do so could cost you the interview and the job.

Preparing Your Résumé

The most popular résumé styles that are used regularly by people in health care professions are the functional and the accomplishment résumés. Both types contain all the standard autobiographical data, such as your name, address, telephone number, education history, and work experiences. They differ in their approach to employment description.

The functional résumé can be advantageous to people who have considerable field experience or to those who are just embarking upon a career in the health care area after being employed in another field for a number of years. The functional résumé features specific jobs a person has held with minimal supplemental information. For example, you might find the following type of item in a functional résumé:

> 1985 to Present: Community Hospital, Charlottesville, N.C. Registered nurse in 20-bed oncology unit. Rendered nursing care, administered chemotherapeutic agents, and provided patient education.

In contrast to the functional résumé, the accomplishment résumé places considerable emphasis upon the applicant's achievements. A typical accomplishment résumé might include the following:

> 1986 to Present. As a registered nurse, developed education program to teach patients how to self-administer chemotherapy and published the article, "Self-Administration of Chemotherapy in the Home."

This type of résumé is more interesting to the employer because actual achievements are listed. By listing your accomplishments, you spell out what you have done in the past and indicate what you are capable of achieving in the future.

Now let us review some of the basic guidelines for developing an effective résumé and place these tips into the "do's and don'ts" of preparing a résumé.

Do's of preparing a résumé:
- Start a permanent résumé file.
- List all your education experience and achievements.
- Know the kind of work you are seeking.
- Be sure to place your name, address, and telephone number at the top of the résumé.
- Give personal information at the end of the résumé.
- Be specific.
- Be quantitative.
- Use action words.
- Keep it short (one or two pages).
- Use good bond, white, or off-white paper.
- Write a cover letter on the same bond paper.
- Check and recheck for typing errors and misspellings.

Don'ts of preparing a résumé:
- Don't include job requirements.
- Don't discuss lack of employment.
- Don't discuss reasons for leaving your present job.
- Don't use gimmicks.
- Don't criticize your former employers.
- Don't include a photograph of yourself.
- Don't use the word "I."
- Don't use abbreviations.

The Cover Letter

Every time you send a résumé to a potential employer you must include a cover letter. Often it is this letter that decides whether you will be granted an interview. The cover letter must be tailored so you will have the competitive edge over other applicants. If you have trouble writing letters, get someone who can write persuasively to help you.

Let us suppose that you have applied for a position as a dietitian at a local hospital. About 20 other people have also applied. Somehow you have to stand apart from the crowd at the outset. You have to grab the employer's attention by using a degree of flair. Your cover letter introduces you to the employer and ideally arrests his or her attention, stimulates interest in you, and convinces the employer that you are the person he or she most wants to interview.

Let us spend some time reviewing the basic elements of a cover letter. First make sure that your name, complete address, telephone number, and the date are in the upper right-hand corner of your cover letter. Do not forget to include your area code, especially if you are applying for a position outside of your local area code.

Next, address the person to whom you are writing by name, if possible. Sometimes you will know the person's name, and other times it will not be listed in the advertisement. Therefore, you may have to use your network if you are to write a personal letter. You could also call the hospital or the organization and request the name of the personnel director or the administrator. Remember, you must gain a favorable impression from the start.

What should you include in the body of the cover letter? This depends on why you are writing a letter in the first place. For example, if a friend or a colleague from your network referred you, you could be writing an unsolicited letter that announces your availability, or you could be answering a publicized job opening. No matter what your reason is, the first thing you must do is establish for the reader exactly why you are writing. In the first sentence you might want to say something like, "I am writing you in response to your advertisement for a dietitian, which was published in *The Philadelphia Inquirer*, July 14."

Successful Interviewing

By now you should be ready for the climax of your job campaign—the interview. You have already realistically assessed your goals, utilized the network, designed an attractive résumé, and written a dynamic cover letter.

If your interview experience is limited or nonexistent, you are probably uncertain or hesitant about what to say or how to say it. To gain practice you can participate in role-playing exercises. Ask a friend to engage in a mock interview session with you.

Most interviewers use a question-and-answer format. Your task is to respond quickly and intelligently. Chances are you will be asked a few personal questions to break the ice. It is safe to assume you will be asked some of these questions: What do you know about our hospital or institution? What can I do for you? What do you consider your strongest skill? Why do you want to join our staff? What will you be doing in five years or ten years? What can you tell me about yourself?

If you are being interviewed on a one-to-one basis, you will have to handle some things differently than if you are being interviewed before a group. As the administrator or the personnel director talks to you, be sure to take notes. Most administrators or people interviewing you believe that note-taking signifies an organized, interested applicant.

Now let's review some of the important elements in handling the interview:

- Practice beforehand.
- Be yourself, not an actor.
- Bring extra copies of your résumé.
- Study your résumé beforehand.
- Tell the interviewers what you can do for them.
- Know and be prepared to discuss three or four of your strongest assets.
- Be specific and to the point.
- Keep to the facts, minimize opinions.
- Never argue with the interviewer.
- Be a good listener.
- Take notes.

Follow-Up and Accepting the Job

The first thing you want to do when you leave the interview is review the notes you took. Even though you may not have been able to jot down everything you wanted to, take the time now to add any important notes that were omitted earlier. For example, if the administrator confided in you that he or she is having a terrible time trying to find a director of nursing who will produce dynamic results, make sure you not only include this tip, but underline it for emphasis. You can capitalize on the situation. Note-taking is very important.

After your interview, you should send handwritten thank-you notes to the people who interviewed you. Thank the interviewers for taking time to meet with you, and tell them how excited you are by this job prospect. This was once the norm when interviewing, but is done less frequently today. However, it is to your benefit to set yourself apart from the competition in the eyes of your interviewer.

You may not always be told why an employer rejected you. If this happens you should contact the administrator or personnel director and ask why you are no longer in the running. Although this may seem like a painful procedure, you need to make every effort to find out exactly what the reasons were for your elimination. What if you lost the job because of insufficient clinical knowledge? If you do not find this out at the start of your job campaign, you can be destroyed in interview after interview. You must be able to correct this gap in your knowledge. Otherwise you will never win a responsible position in health care.

Appendix A

Common Medical Abbreviations and Acronyms

AABB: American Association of Blood Banks
A.D.: Associate Degree
ADA: American Dietetic Association
AHA: American Hospital Association
AMA: American Medical Association
ANA: American Nurses Association
BC/BS: Blue Cross/Blue Shield
CDC: Centers for Disease Control
CEO: Chief Executive Officer
CFO: Chief Financial Officer
C.N.M.: Certified Nurse Midwife
C.R.N.A.: Certified Registered Nurse Anesthetist
CRO: Chief Resource Officer (Purchasing
    Director/Materials Manager)
DHHS: Department of Health and Human Services
D.M.D.: Doctor of Dental Medicine
D.O.: Doctor of Osteopathy

ECF: Extended Care Facility
EDP: Electronic Data Processing
EMS: Emergency Medical Services
E.M.T.: Emergency Medical Technician
ER: Emergency Room
FMG: Foreign Medical Graduate
F.P.: Family Practitioner
FTE: Full-Time Equivalent
G.P.: General Practitioner
GYN: Gynecology
HCFA: Health Care Financing Administration
HHA: Home Health Agency
ICF: Intermediate Care Facility
ICU: Intensive Care Unit
IDS: Integrated Delivery System
JCAHO: Joint Commission on Accreditation Healthcare
    Organizations
LTC: Long-Term Care
L.V.N.: Licensed Vocational Nurse/Licensed Practical
    Nurse
MA: Medical Audit
M.B.A. : Master's of Business Administration
MCO: Managed Care Organization
M.D.: Doctor of Medicine
M.R.T.: Medical Records Technician
M.T.: Medical Technologist
N.A.: Nursing Assistant
NIH: National Institutes of Health
NLN: National League for Nursing
NMRI: Nuclear Magnetic Resonance Imaging
O.M.T.: Ophthalmic Medical Technician

OR: Operating Room
OT: Occupational Therapist
P.A.: Physician Assistant
PACE: Program of All-Inclusive Care for the Elderly
PC: Personal Computer
P.C.P.: Primary Care Physician
PHS: Public Health Service
PRO: Peer Review Organization
PT: Physical Therapy
QA: Quality Assurance Program
QM: Quality Management
RAD: Radiographer
RADTT: Radiation Therapy Technologist
R.D.: Registered Dietitian
R.N.: Registered Nurse
R.R.A.: Registered Record Administrator
R.R.T.: Registered Respiratory Therapist
Rx: Prescription and Treatment
SAS: Specific Activity Scale
SNF: Skilled Nursing Facility
SSA: Social Security Administration
S.T.: Surgical Technologist
Title XVIII: Medicare
Title XIX: Medicaid
TQM: Total Quality Management
UR: Utilization Review
USPHS: United States Public Health Service
VA: Veterans Administration
V.M.D.: Doctor of Veterinary Medicine
VNA: Visiting Nurses Association
WHO: World Health Organization

Appendix B

Facilities, Services, and Programs Where Health Care Workers Are Employed

Adult Day Care Program
Alcoholism/Drug Abuse or Dependency Inpatient Unit
Alcoholism/Drug Abuse or Dependency Outpatient
    Services
Ambulance Services
Ambulatory Surgicenters
Angioplasty
Arthritis Treatment Center
Assisted Living/Personal Care
Birthing Room/LDR Room/LDRP Room
Blood Banks
Breast Cancer Screening/Mammograms
Burn Care Unit
Cancer Centers
Cardiac Catheterization Laboratory
Cardiac Intensive Care Unit
Case Management

Chaplaincy/Pastoral Care Services
Children Wellness Program
Clinical Laboratories
Community Health Reporting
Community Health Status Assessment
Community Health-Status-Based Service Planning
Community Mental Health Centers
Community Outreach Activities
Congregate Care
Continuing Care Retirement Communities
Crisis and Prevention Centers
CT Scanner
Dental Group Practices and Dental Services
Diagnostic Imaging Facility
Emergency Department Services
Extracorporeal Shock Wave Lithotripter
Facilities for the Deaf or Blind
Facilities for the Emotionally Disturbed
Facilities for the Mentally Retarded
Family Planning Clinics
Freestanding Outpatient Care Center
Geriatric Assessment Services
Health Facility Transportation (to/from)
Health Fairs/Promotion/Screenings
Health Information Center
Health Maintenance Organizations
HIV/AIDS Services
Home Health Services
Hospice
Hospital-Based Outpatient Care Center-Services

Magnetic Resonance Imaging (MRI)
Meals on Wheels
Medical Surgical Intensive Care Unit
Migrant Workers Health Projects
Neighborhood Health Centers
Neonatal Intensive Care Unit
Nursing Home—Intermediate Care
Nursing Home—Skilled Care
Nutrition Programs
Obstetrics Unit
Occupational Health Services
Oncology Services
Open-Heart Surgery
Organ/Tissue Transplant
Outpatient Surgery
Patient Education Center
Patient Representative Services
Pediatric Intensive Care Unit
Physical Rehabilitation Inpatient Unit
Physical Rehabilitation Outpatient Services
Poison Control Centers
Positron Emission Tomography Scanner (PET)
Psychiatric Acute Inpatient Unit
Psychiatric Child Adolescent Services
Psychiatric Consultation—Liaison Services
Psychiatric Education Services
Psychiatric Emergency Services
Psychiatric Geriatric Services
Psychiatric Outpatient Services
Psychiatric Partial Hospitalization Program

Radiation Therapy
Renal Disease Treatment Centers
Reproductive Health Services (fertility counseling, in vitro
    fertilization, sterilization)
Respite Care
Single Photon Emission Computerized Tomography
    (SPECT)
Skilled Nursing Hospital Long-Term Care Unit
Social Work Services
Specialized Outpatient Program for HIV/AIDS
Sports Medicine
Support Groups
Transplant Services
Trauma Center (certified)
Work Site Health Promotion

Glossary of Selected Health and Medical Terms

Accreditation. A process that a third-party reviewer uses to evaluate health facilities, services, and programs, including the quality of patient care.

Administrators. Institutional and organizational executives in the health care system. The institutions employing such individuals range from group practice clinics to the largest medical centers. Organizations include local long-term care facilities, insurance plans, and governmental programs.

Allopathy. Conventional medical practice that deals with the treatment and prevention of disease.

Ambulatory Care. Refers to medical or health services given on an outpatient basis. It usually implies that the patient was ambulatory and came to the facility where the services were offered.

Bed. A bed found in a hospital or nursing home used for patients. Beds are used as a measure of an institution's capacity and size.

Blue Cross/Blue Shield. A combined insurance plan: Blue Cross for hospitalization, Blue Shield for physician services. Most subscribers enroll at their place of employment in group plans.

Board of Trustees (also called Board of Directors, Governing Boards). The ultimate authority in a hospital or health institution. The board represents the community and is the policy-making body of the institution.

Catastrophic Care. Medical services that are provided for prolonged critical illnesses or injuries.

Certification. The process by which a government agency, a non-government agency, or a health-related association evaluates and recognizes an individual, institution, program, service, or an educational program as meeting predetermined standards.

Chronic Illness. An illness that has been continuing for a long period of time and may recur over a long period of time. Alterations in such illnesses are slow.

Clinic Patients. Outpatients who use either the services of a hospital, which may be offered at a reduced rate, or those offered at private clinics at regular charges.

Clinical. A term relating to direct contact with or information observed by a physician, nurse, or other health care provider about a patient's course of illness.

Clinical Privileges. A permission granted to a practitioner that enables him or her to render specific diagnostic, therapeutic, medical, nursing, dental, podiatric, or surgical services.

Community Health Center. An organization and institution established in a residential community to offer a range of public and private health services.

Community Hospital. A hospital established to meet the medical needs of a specific geographical area. Generally they are not-for-profit hospitals, but they may also be proprietary hospitals.

Continuing Education. Formal education that is obtained by a health professional after completing a bachelor's degree or post-graduate training. This education is intended to improve or maintain the professional's competence.

Credentials. The documents and certificates issued in recognition of professional or technical competence.

Department. A unit within a hospital, nursing home, or other institution that has a specific functional responsibility in that facility, for example, the nursing department or the housekeeping department.

Doctor. Any person with a doctoral degree. Sometimes used synonymously for a physician.

Emergency Patients. Outpatients who are usually acutely ill and use a hospital or freestanding emergency department for treatment.

Extended-Care Facility. An institution that provides care to patients who do not require full active hospital care. Nursing homes and rehabilitation hospitals are examples of an extended-care facility.

Facilities. Those physical entities such as the physical plant, equipment, and supplies that are required to carry out the mission of an institution or organization.

Fee for Service Payment. A charge for a type (or unit) of medical service rendered. Reimbursement is made only for those services that are actually rendered.

Flexner Report. A survey by the Carnegie Foundation, published in 1910, to evaluate medical education in the United States. The report found the quality of education to be so poor that within 18 months of its publication more than half of the medical schools in the country had closed permanently. Abraham Flexner, from whom it received its name, headed the survey team.

Foreign Medical Graduate (FMG). A physician who graduated from medical school outside the United States. U.S. citizens who go to medical school outside this country are classified as foreign medical graduates just as foreign-born persons who are not trained in medical schools in this country are classified.

Geriatrics. That branch of medicine that treats all conditions particular to old age and the aging process.

Government Hospitals. Hospitals that are owned by local, state, or federal government.

Group Practice. A formal association of physicians providing either specialty or comprehensive medical care on an outpatient basis.

Head Nurse. The nurse in charge of a specific nursing unit, usually in a hospital, nursing home, or other health care organization. The head nurse is responsible for the activities of the unit over 24 hours per day, seven days per week.

Health Administration. The management of resources, procedures, and systems that operate to meet the needs and wants in the health care system.

Health and Human Services. A department of the federal government that originally was part of the Department of Health, Education and Welfare, established in 1935. This department coordinates the following agencies: the Food and Drug Administration; Office of Human Development; Public Health Service; Social Security Administration; Alcohol, Drug Abuse, and Mental Health Administration; National Institutes of Health; Centers for Disease Control; Health Care Financing Administration; Office of Child Support; and the Office of Smoking and Health. In 1979 a separate Department of Education was established, and the remainder of the Department of Health, Education, and Welfare became the Department of Health and Human Services.

Health Maintenance Organization (HMO). A system to provide health care, usually based on a prepayment method. HMOs are responsible for providing most health and medical services for the individual and family.

Health and Medical Care System. The institutions and resources that work together to deliver health services, including medical care services, community health services, and personal health services.

Health Planning. Planning concerned with improving the community's health. It may involve a particular population, type of service, or institution.

Health Professionals. Physicians, nurses, and other health care providers who are sources of support and information on diagnosis, treatment, or prevention of an illness or injury.

Health Systems Agency (HSA). A health planning and resources development agency that is designated under the terms of the National Health Planning and Resources Development Act of

1974, public law 93-641. HSAs are nonprofit, private corporations or public regional planning bodies that are charged with performing the health planning and resources development functions for a geographical area. HSAs replaced the comprehensive health planning agencies and had expanded duties and powers.

Health Team. An organization of health practitioners who represent various professions and work cooperatively in planning and rendering health care services.

Holistic. An approach to the study of an individual in totality rather than in the aggregate of separate physiological, psychological, and social characteristics.

Home Health Agency. Organizations that provide nursing, medical, and health services in the patient's home. These organizations may be private or public.

Homeopathy. A system of medicine expounded by Samuel Hahnemann. This system states that the inflicted person should be given minute doses of remedies that produce the same signs and symptoms in a healthy person. This is said to stimulate body defenses against the signs and the symptoms of the disease. A practitioner of homeopathy is called a homeopath.

Hospital. An institution that provides medical and health care around the clock, seven days a week.

Industrial Medicine. That branch of medicine concerned with the injuries, illnesses, and diseases that occur to an employee working in his or her occupation. It focuses on the prevention of disease in industry rather than on creating optimal health and productivity and social adjustment within industry. Illnesses that occur within industrial medicine are commonly called industrial diseases. Synonym: occupational medicine.

Inpatient. An individual housed in a hospital overnight to receive medical treatment.

Institution. Either a private or public entity or organization established for a certain purpose.

Job Description. A summary of the key features, elements, or requirements of a certain specific job category. This summary is generally written after a review of the job, called a job analysis.

Laboratory. A place where clinical specimens are tested and the results obtained and recorded. Synonym: clinical laboratory.

License. Permission that is granted to an individual or organization by competent authority, usually public, to enable the person or organization to engage in a practice, occupation, or activity that is otherwise unlawful.

Long-Term Care Institution. An organization established for the care of patients for a prolonged period of time, usually greater than 30 days. Care given may include medical, nursing, and other supportive care.

Medical Ethics. A set of principles that govern conduct in the medical and physician community. The principles involve such areas as a physician's relationship to a patient, the patient's family, fellow physicians, as well as to society at large.

Medical Services. Services of a medical nature offered to patients at their request and rendered by physicians, dentists, nurses, or other health professionals.

Nursing Care Unit. An organized entity within the nursing service of a hospital or nursing home in which continuous nursing care is provided.

Nursing Homes. A broad range of institutions excluding hospitals. These institutions provide a wide variety of services and levels of care, ranging from skilled nursing to custodial care.

Nursing Service. Patient care services pertaining to the curative, restorative, and preventive aspects of nursing. These are performed and supervised by a registered nurse pursuant to the medical care plan of the practitioner or nursing care plan.

Outpatient. An individual who receives hospital services in a clinic, emergency department, or other hospital facility and who is not admitted as an inpatient.

Primary Care. Professional and related services that are administered by a practitioner with referral to a secondary care specialist when necessary. The care may involve preventive, diagnostic, therapeutic, rehabilitative, or palliative services.

Proprietary Hospital. A medical care facility offering inpatient services. It is owned privately and operated for profit.

Public Health. A broad area of health that refers to the physical problems of individuals and to the network of factors—biological, socioeconomic, and psychological—that affect the community.

Sheltered-Care Institutions. Facilities that provide permanent accommodations for residents and that offer health and medical services occasionally as needed; for example, a life-care community program.

Teaching Hospital. A hospital usually associated with a medical school that offers formal medical teaching programs for interns and residents.

Technician. A person who specializes in the technical details of a process, e.g. biomedical technician.

Therapist. An individual whose knowledge and skills enable him or her to prevent or correct physical, mental, or developmental disorders as well as to provide services that will improve or enhance the person's physical or mental well-being. Three or more years of educational preparation are usually necessary to acquire the basic competency in a given therapy.

About the Authors

I. **Donald Snook** was a nationally renowned leader in hospital management and marketing and was the president of Presbyterian Foundation for Philadelphia. Prior to assuming this position, he was CEO of Presbyterian Medical Center of Philadelphia.

Dr. Snook contributed more than 60 articles to health care management literature and authored several books, including the widely read *Hospitals: What They Are and How They Work*. His last work was *Child of Providence: A History of Presbyterian Hospital in Philadelphia*, written in 1996. He was the originator of the "hotel-hospital" concept. He was the recipient of the American Healthcare Marketing Association's CEO Marketer of the Year Award and received the Senior Regent Award from the ACHE's southeastern Pennsylvania region.

Dr. Snook held a B.B.A. in marketing from the Wharton School of the University of Pennsylvania (cum laude) and an M.B.A. in hospital administration from George Washington University. He also completed the Health Management Systems Program at the Harvard Business School. He earned his Ph.D. from the University of Pennsylvania.

Dr. Snook was a faculty member in the graduate program in health care administration at LaSalle and Penn State universities, and was a fellow in the American College of Healthcare Executives. Dr. Snook presented more than 450 lectures and seminars nationally on contemporary issues.

LEO PAUL D'ORAZIO, M.B.A., C.H.E., a leading health care authority in the Northeast, is currently managing director of health care for Withum, Smith, and Brown, a top 30 CPA and consulting firm based in New Jersey. Mr. D'Orazio was formerly the senior vice president/COO of Integrated Delivery Systems for the Taylor Hospital Foundation, Ridley Park, Pennsylvania.

A health care consultant and administrator for 31 years, Mr. D'Orazio began his career in 1973 working for the personnel department of Mercy Catholic Medical Center, Darby. He left seven years later to serve as senior vice president and assistant administrator for St. Mary Hospital, Philadelphia. In 1985 he joined the Northwestern Institute of Psychiatry, Fort Washington, as chief executive officer. The following year Mr. D'Orazio became principal-in-charge of Arthur Young and Company's health care consulting practice in Philadelphia. He also served as vice president of Garofolo, Curtis, and Company, Ardmore, Pennsylvania. He spent the next five and one-half years as the health care partner-in-charge for Zelenkofske, Axelrod, and Company, Ltd., a national health care, consulting, and public accounting firm.

Mr. D'Orazio holds a B.A. in business administration from West Chester University and an M.B.A. in health care administration from Temple University. He is a member of the American Hospital Association, the Hospital Association of Pennsylvania, the Healthcare Financial Management Association, and a diplomate in the American College of Healthcare Executives. He has served as president of Temple University's M.B.A. Department of Health Administration Alumni Association. He has held faculty appointments at Temple University, LaSalle University, University of St. Francis, Thomas Jefferson University, and Wilmington College and teaches both undergraduate and graduate courses in health care administration. Mr. D'Orazio is a former chairperson of the board, president, vice president, and treasurer of the Society for Advancement of Management.

Mr. D'Orazio has made presentations on numerous topics for the American College of Health Care Executives, American Hospital Association, the Hospital Association of Pennsylvania, National Association of Radiology Technologists, Greater Philadelphia Health Assembly, and the Temple University Department of Health Administration Continuing Education Institute. He is currently a diplomate in the American College of Health Care Executives.